From the Library of

_____

ASSAULT
on
LIBERTY

Rebirth of the "Fairness Doctrine"

BY DR. KENNETH C. HILL

Foreword by Dr. Larry Bates

ASSAULT ON LIBERTY
The Rebirth of the "FAIRNESS DOCTRINE"

ISBN 978-0-9801152-1-5

Dedication:

To my Father and Mother, Clyde and Erma Hill, who introduced me
to the freedom I have in Jesus Christ.

To Ministers of the Gospel who have proclaimed freedom in Jesus
Christ in times of adversity, and
To the Broadcasters who have aided them
in this noble task of proclamation.

Acknowledgments:

A word of thanks is in order for Cheryl Senter who assisted
with typing and proofing the text, and to Marilyn Brannan
for her editorial skills.

Sincere Thanks To:
Dr. Don Smith of the Radio Bible Hour (www.radiobiblehour.org)

Howard and Marlie Barnawell, who gave me
my first introduction to the J. Harold Smith saga

And to the many others, too numerous to mention individually, who
have helped in the preparation of this project.

FOREWORD

By Dr. Larry Bates

In the years following the founding of the United States of America, which emanated from the fires of liberty burning in the hearts of early patriots, the Declaration of Independence and the Constitutional Convention of 1787 provided a framework of government based on self-government. Our nation was founded on the premise that we would restrict ourselves, conduct ourselves, and control ourselves according to the Ten Commandments of God. The Constitution and statute books were to retreat to the "corner"—to be operative only for heathens and those believers who had lost sight of their responsibilities under God's laws.

Our framework of checks and balances imbedded in the founding documents spread power among the three branches (executive, legislative, judicial) of the federal government. Limited powers were enumerated to the federal government, and the rest of the power was delegated to the states and the people respectively. In other words, the public officials governed with the consent of the governed. The Bill of Rights was not a restriction upon the people, but rather, a restriction upon government. Specifically, the First Amendment reads in part, "Congress shall make no law . . . abridging the freedom of speech, or of the press." In fact, the press was often referred to as the "fourth estate," or the fourth branch looking over and informing the public of the activities of the public officials in the three branches of government.

Throughout history, there has been a lust for power among kings and rulers. The dustbins of history are filled with accounts of tyrants and despots who abused their powers. America has prospered from, and has been greatly blessed by, her unique form of self-government. However, we are presently at a crossroads in the "valley of decision." Our action—or lack of action—will determine the future of our system of government.

As an economist and former legislator, I have witnessed first-hand the battles for political power. The volume of political "spin" and propaganda, especially at election time, is overwhelming. The Prophet Hosea lamented in Hosea 4:6, "My people are destroyed for lack of knowledge." And we read in John 8:32: "and ye shall know the truth and the truth shall make you free." It is not the truth that makes us free; it is our knowledge of the truth that makes us free.

In *Assault on Liberty, Rebirth of the Fairness Doctrine*, Dr. Kenneth Hill shows you how politicians and government officials are attempting to stifle those messengers they consider "controversial," and silence those messages that expose them to the light of public scrutiny.

If the "Fairness Doctrine" is resurrected, the result will not be easier access for controversial or opposing views. Instead, broadcast stations, out of fear, will impose self-censorship by airing nothing that could be considered controversial. The free marketplace of views and ideas, including the "controversial" Gospel of Jesus Christ, will be non-existent.

Dr. Hill shows you in this book the history and application of the so-called Fairness Doctrine—and how the enemies of liberty have attempted, through the use of that Doctrine, to put listeners in total darkness. He further shows that in a broadcast environment protected by the First Amendment, there is a simple solution for an individual looking for an alternative viewpoint, or for a politician "offended" by a talk show host: Turn the dial.

It is estimated that approximately 40% of Americans get their news and information from talk radio. To assault free speech with the "Fairness Doctrine" would be a serious blow to the future of freedom and liberty in the USA. It is time to resist these politicians who would seek to further empower themselves while enslaving the rest of us. Spread the word.

Dr. Larry Bates, CEO
Information Radio Network
IRN/USA Radio News

PREFACE

Why should YOU be concerned about free speech and the "Fairness Doctrine"?

This book explains why. The "Fairness Doctrine" was once used by the Federal Communications Commission to silence broadcasters who dared to challenge—by name and deed—the enemies of the Gospel.

The Fairness Doctrine was abolished in 1987. Since its demise, however, liberals in Congress have attempted to revive the Doctrine and its abuses. The effort has gained strength as liberals have gained power in much of Washington.

If it is reinstated, the Fairness Doctrine will be used as the liberals' weapon of choice to limit the freedom of broadcasters to keep you informed about what the enemy of our souls and his agents are doing to keep the truth of the Gospel from being preached throughout our land.

--Dr. Kenneth C. Hill

CONTENTS

Appendices

CHAPTER

1

Why Should Anyone Be Interested in the "Fairness Doctrine"?

L et me begin by emphasizing that the "Fairness Doctrine" was never intended to be *fair* or lead to *fairness* in broadcasting. It was conceived as a method of taming the conversation of the broadcaster and placing a chill upon the broadcaster in order to effect a silencing of the truth. –Dr. Kenneth C. Hill

The assault on virtually every right guaranteed to citizens of the United States of America under the Constitution has been underway since the founding of our Republic. The subject of this book is the right of free speech in America and how—and why—that right suffered egregious assault in this nation for a period of 38 years under the so-called "Fairness Doctrine."

Thankfully, the forces that suppressed freedom of speech under that doctrine (which actually was not a *law*, but a *bureaucratic ruling* instituted by the Federal Communications Commission in 1949) were dealt a severe blow in 1987 when the doctrine was repealed during the Reagan administration.

Unfortunately, those elements of our society who would deny freedom of speech to the opposition—that is, anyone with different political, religious, or ideological views—are again at work in Congress and in numerous public milieus to revive the "Fairness Doctrine."

It is critically important for Americans to know the truth about the history of the "Fairness Doctrine" and to be aware of the efforts for its reinstatement. The story, once told, requires vigilance on the part of each person who loves the freedoms that are enumerated in our Constitution and Bill of Rights. This assault must be repelled for the future well being of our nation. It is *my* responsibility, and it is *your* responsibility.

In the chapters of this book that follow, I will give you the facts of the mechanism that governs broadcasting in these United States: the Federal Communications Commission. I will present the history of the "Fairness Doctrine," and I will attempt to assist you in understanding the reasons for its inception and why it was abolished. It is my hope that, through reading this book, you will come to understand the forces at work to deprive you of your freedom to speak—and to hear—the truth. You will be challenged to use your knowledge to protect our nation.

As you move through the chapters of this book, I urge you to keep uppermost in your mind two salient and powerful truths:

> *Number 1:* Our Constitution *guarantees* the right of free speech to every American. The First Amendment to the Constitution of the United States of America states, *"Congress shall make no law* respecting an establishment of religion, or prohibiting the free exercise thereof; or *abridging the freedom of speech, or of the press*; or the right of the people peaceably to assemble, and to petition the government for a redress of grievances."

> *Number 2:* The Holy Bible explains, in one short statement by Jesus Christ Our Lord, why we must make it a lifelong mission to seek the truth. Jesus said,

>

> *"Ye shall know the truth,*
> *and the truth shall make you free"* (John 8:32).

>

CHAPTER

2

The Federal Communications Commission

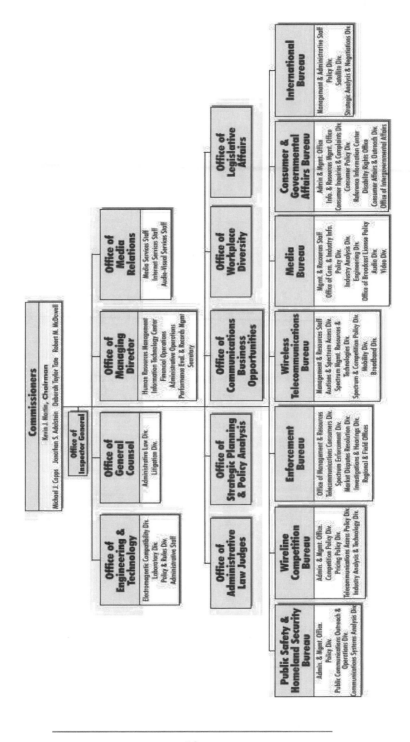

When we seek to understand the forces at work in the suppression of free speech on the airwaves, we must first look at those who regulate radio and television in the United States. Let's begin with an introduction to the bulging bureaucracy that controls every word that is uttered and every picture transmitted on the public airwaves—the Federal Communications Commission.

The Federal Communications Commission (FCC) was established with the Communications Act of 1934 to be the independent United States government agency directly responsible to Congress for the regulation of communications. The FCC's mandate from Congress is to regulate interstate and international communications by radio, television, wire, satellite, and cable for all the States, the District of Columbia, and all possessions of the United States.

Although there were more members of the FCC in the past, today the Commission is directed by five Commissioners who are appointed by the President and confirmed by the Senate. These Appointees serve five-year terms. It is the President who designates the Chairman of the FCC and it is normal for the Chairman to be of the President's political party. No more than three Commissioners may be from any one political party.

The Commission staff is organized by function. There are seven operating Bureaus and ten Staff Offices. The Media Bureau regulates all radio and television broadcast stations as well as cable and satellite services to the general public.

While the FCC is charged with the regulation of the various forms of electronic communication, in reality they do not regulate much more than the economics of such communication. The present Commissioners have *no background in the workings of the broadcast industry* (see Appendix VII - Members of the Federal Commissions Commission). They are bureaucrats of the first order, with law degrees and backgrounds in various types of regulatory agencies or lobbying firms. Most display an understanding of regulation of common carriers, but *no* understanding of issues pertaining to public broadcast and cable media.

At this point in our discussion, you need to know that the FCC views all public communication types as the same. In other words (in the view of the FCC), the cell phones provide the same service as the cable—as does the satellite radio—as does broadcast radio and television. Former FCC Chairman, Mark Fowler, once called television "a toaster with pictures." That's ridiculous.

Consider your use of the cell phone. If you are in the "now" generation, the cell phone is your main personal communication device. It is used for sending/receiving texts, photos, music, downloads, uploads, gaming, calendar, alarms, and of course conversation.

What about the cable service? Does it simply bring in over-the-air television into your home or office? Of course not. It brings in HD and analog signals from local and faraway broadcast stations; but it also brings in satellite channels, pay-per-view, limited access, and other video. Don't forget the music channels, and of course, there is telephone service and internet access. The broadband services are practically limitless.

Have you listened to satellite radio? Does it give you the same services as the cable company or the cell phone industry?

And then there is the granddaddy of all the mass communication media—over-the-air, or terrestrial, broadcasting. This includes television and radio that is received by the individual consumer on an individual receiving set. Most people receive their television through a cable service, although they still can receive their local channels without the cable.

Over-the-air radio and television do not provide the same services as cellular, satellite, cable, and other media. These two provide similar services to the public, but in different forms. Television provides visual entertainment and information in an impersonal fashion. Radio, on the other hand, is a personal medium. We listen to radio in the car, when we are at work, when wanting to relax or wanting to be informed. One might say that radio is a *companion*, while television is a *visitor.*

Well-informed Public: Anathema to Out-of-step Government

Although the FCC professes to believe that all modes of communication are the same and should be regulated without differentiation, that is not true when it comes to content regulation. Until the repeal of the "Fairness Doctrine" the only communication segments to be controlled by the FCC were broadcast radio and television.

Today, broadcast radio and television are still the only services regulated by the FCC that are screened for content. *Why?* Because of two significant facts that lie at the very heart of the matter: (1) *broadcast radio and television are enormously powerful communications tools;* and (2) *a government that is not in step with, and responsive to, its people fears a well-informed public.*

Should the "Fairness Doctrine" be re-created as it has been proposed, it will impact only television and over-the-air radio. But—if the FCC really believed (as they profess) that all media should be regulated equally, then they would place the same content restrictions on satellite radio, satellite television, cable channels and the rest.

In view of this glaring discrepancy between what the FCC professes and what it actually enforces as policy, it becomes obvious that *political* considerations—not good public policy—are the forces that have governed FCC content regulation.

3

Recent Bureaucratic Blunders by the FCC

The DTV Transition Blunder

The FCC has further demonstrated its lack of understanding of the differences in the various communication domains, which they control when they chart a course that does not include broadcast radio and television as a dominant media force. The Congress and the FCC made a huge blunder when they mandated the change from analog to digital transmission by the nation's TV stations. They even set a certain date, February 17, 2009, as the time when all analog transmission will be terminated. The idea of the government was to grab tens of billions of dollars through the sale of the analog spectrum. They really didn't think there would be much of a problem with the viewing public.

Then reality dawned and the Congress and the FCC began to work to give each other cover so the public would not be upset at the prospect of buying new television sets because their old ones had been made obsolete overnight. Billions of consumer dollars will be spent on the transition. The broadcasters were forced to spend two to three million dollars per station to place the digital signal on the air. They have no place to use the analog equipment, so they had to write it off as their loss. All of this, because the Federal Government wanted more money for their schemes.

In an article by Diane Mermigas in the November 29, 2005 edition of "The Hollywood Reporter," we find the following:

> " . . . the trashing of about 300 million TV sets suddenly rendered technologically obsolete would have a brutal environmental impact. The alternative is $10 billion-$12 billion in upgrades, or a $50-$60 converter for the estimated 200 million of those TV sets with no digital capacity . . .

> " . . . Congress has discussed modest government subsidies of one-third the $750 million-$900 million cost to provide one conversion device to each of the country's estimated 15 million over-the-air-only households . . .

" . . . Regardless of how it comes down, the one group expected to be disproportionately disadvantaged are the owners of the nation's roughly 1,750 full-power commercial and public TV stations, who have spent an average $2 million-$3 million per outlet to upgrade analog facilities . . ."

The government web site set up to diffuse consumer wrath is http://www.dtv2009.gov. Your government is offering a $40 coupon to help with the purchase of a converter box to enable the digital signal to be received.

At that site we read: "What is the digital television transition? At midnight on February 17, 2009, all full-power television stations in the United States will stop broadcasting in analog and switch to 100% digital broadcasting. Digital broadcasting promises to provide a clearer picture and more programming options and will free up airwaves for use by emergency responders."

Billions to U.S. Treasury from Confiscated Broadcast Spectrum

Yes, emergency responders will get a very small slice of the frequencies that will become available. However, you should note that the government does not tell the whole truth. They omit information about the multiplied billions of dollars expected to flow to the United States' Treasury from auctioning of the confiscated broadcast spectrum.

Prior to the mid-1990's, telecommunications companies were lobbying the FCC to force some television licensees to move to other frequencies so they could use the space for other communication uses. Now the stage is set by the removal of all analog television broadcasting from the nation. The auction of the former analog television "channels" will create massive amounts of new business in various broadband and wireless business, and the Federal Government expects a large piece of the action.

The site also states: "Congress created the TV Converter Box Coupon

Program for households wishing to keep using their analog TV sets after February 17, 2009. The Program allows U.S. households to obtain up to two coupons, each worth $40, that can be applied toward the cost of eligible converter boxes. A TV connected to cable, satellite or other pay TV service does not require a TV converter box from this program.

"Consumers have a variety of options. Options to explore include:
1. Keep your existing analog TV and purchase a TV converter box. A converter box plugs into your TV and will keep it working after Feb. 17, 2009; or
2. Connect to cable, satellite or other pay service; or
3. Purchase a television with a digital tuner."

The Congress is beginning to show its concern for an ill-conceived transition. In an article published July 30, 2007 in Broadcast Engineering, we read:

At a Senate hearing last week, legislators made it clear they have little trust in the government or television broadcasters to pull off a successful transition.

Senator Daniel Inouye (D-HI) said the government needs to act "before the digital transition devolves into digital disaster." There is a "high potential for a train wreck here," said Senator Maria Cantwell, (D-WA). Without a better educational effort, the government could have "a disaster on our hands," said Sen. Olympia J. Snowe, (R-ME).

"It's not the government or broadcasters who are going to feel the heat, but the nation's elected representatives," said Senator Claire McCaskill, (D-MO). "They're not going to call you," she told the administration bureaucrat handling the transition. "They're going to call me. And they're going to be mad."

There were repeated warnings that the $5 million being spent by the government to educate the public about the digital transition is not nearly enough.

"Consumers will be confused, frustrated, and angry that this important information and entertainment source in their household is no longer operational, through no fault of their own," said Nelda Barnett, a board member of the AARP, the senior citizens advocacy group. "Thousands of telephones will ring in communities around the country as well as right here in hundreds of congressional offices. Constituents will call their elected officials to complain and ask, 'What has happened to my television set?'"

The American public is becoming aware of the situation as detailed in a September 24, 2007 press release from the Association of Public Television Stations:

A recent survey by the Association of Public Television Stations (APTS) finds a majority of Americans feel that the federal government is on the "wrong track" in moving the digital transition forward.

…The survey revealed that the level of disapproval with what is being expected of consumers as part of the transition was essentially the same regardless of the level of consumer awareness. Specifically, 55.7 percent of consumers who are unaware of the transition, and 54.7 percent of consumers who are aware of the transition, say that the government is on the "wrong track."

"The federal government mandated the transition to digital but has failed to make the case to the American public for the decision," said APTS President and CEO John Lawson. "The survey suggests that the efforts of broadcasters and the DTV Transition Coalition are having a positive impact, with the percentage of Americans who were unaware of the DTV transition declining from 61.2 percent in November 2006 to 51.3 percent in August 2007. . . .

"The Federal government stands to reap billions of dollars from the transition, but they have invested less than $10 million in consumer education…"

At a September 19, 2007 hearing before the Senate Special Committee on Aging, Mark Goldstein, Director of Physical Infrastructure Issues at the U.S. Government Accountability Office (GAO), also concluded that the federal government is drastically unprepared to educate the public, particularly seniors, about the transition.

John Lawson added, " . . .The government must devote real resources to raise awareness and make their case to avoid a voter backlash in February 2009. The percentage of respondents who indicated that they were 'very much aware' of the transition increased from 7.8 percent in November 2006 to 19.8 percent in August 2007."

Be aware that the Association of Public Television Stations is the trade association for the government-funded PBS stations who have received hundreds of millions of dollars in support for the transition.

When you consider the hundreds of millions of dollars already spent by the broadcast TV stations to build the digital transmission systems, the multiplied millions spent by the broadcasters in announcing the transition in the hope that consumers will have TV sets in place to receive the new signals, the 1.5 billion dollars expected to be spent by the government in its various attempts to appease the masses affected by this change, the billions spent—and yet to be spent—by consumers to acquire new TV sets, and the hundreds of millions spent by the Federal Government to equip the PBS television stations around the country, it adds up to real money!

All of these expenditures aside, the bottom line is that the individual who receives local news and information from the local television station will be harmed by the transition. This is another limitation of the free flow of information to the consumer.

The Digital Radio (IBOC or HDRadio) Blunder

Before I leave the discussion of the bureaucrats who have oversight of the broadcast stations, I need to mention another decision they have recently made that will be detrimental to the listener of local radio. This is the adoption of the Ibiquity Corporation's IBOC or HDRadio concept for digital radio transmission.

Many years ago, the vision was expressed to create a grand digital broadcasting scheme to aid the AM portion of the radio band. AM radio has suffered from much interference, minimized bandwidth, and noisy reception. This digital domain for the AM stations would allow it to sound like an FM signal with clear signal and lack of noise.

Something happened along the way and the vision has never been achieved. In fact, the FM broadcaster received a digital solution that apparently works, although very few can hear it due to the few receivers on the market. But the vision was not to make FM better; it was to bring AM radio up to the standards already set by the FM system of transmission. This vision was lost.

A number of engineers have told this author that the AM reception could be greatly improved if simple changes were made in the radio receivers being manufactured in these modern times. In other words, the technology is available for dramatic improvement by changing a few electronic components. It has been known by AM broadcast engineers that the radio receiver manufacturers spent more money on improving the FM side of the radio band, while neglecting to improve AM reception.

Meanwhile, the digital radio technology for AM radio has been developed. Unfortunately, the IBOC (HDRadio) system is full of troubles for engineers and listeners alike.

This digital scheme has flaws in the AM transmission system, according to John Battison, writing for beradio.com in May, 2002: "The NRSC report on AM IBOC recommends to the FCC that AM IBOC be approved for daytime use. The daytime service is comparable to FM; but at night, due to first-and second-adjacent channel interference problems, AM IBOC is not recommended. . . . The daytime signal suffers from noise problems, interference, and infringing AM signals . . ."

More recent results following the FCC approval of day and night AM IBOC digital transmission prompted these editorial comments from http://www.am-dx.com:

> "I have had two HD Radios, and found that the digital signals are very fragile, and cover about half the radius (1/4 the area) of a good analog signal. Electrical noise from many sources like car ignition, light dimmers and bad wiring can easily disrupt things.

> "I saw an interesting comment (name and location deleted to protect the writer): "The latest email from xxxxxx in xxxxxx said that the reason the big boys in the big markets are so pro-IBOC is because they like the hash, as it wipes out distant signals getting into their market. There is no way to stop skip, but if the IBOC hash wipes the signal out, then the locals will have to listen to their local station. Kind of like "legal" jamming. Considering that, then even if the public does not buy the radios, keeping the IBOC signal might be worth their while."

> "Jamming is illegal in many ways. If some entity has manipulated this process to allow it, then appropriate action should be taken to shut it off . . ."

> "There are some stations that have directional arrays that may never be able to be compliant with the specs for IBOC transmission. As a result, they will not be able to run it. Is it fair that some can and some cannot be digital? If digital-only operations are mandated, will these stations be forced to go dark? Is that fair to their communities? It would seem that many small town stations cannot afford the license nor the technical upgrades. Again, if digital is mandated, do these small towns simply lose their station, even if it is the only one? That seems grossly unfair."

"Customers are staying away from these radios. Market penetration is very much below the radar. They hope to sell two million HD Radios by the year 2010. That's about how many iPods sell in a month."

" . . . HD Radio is obsolete right out of the box."

"From a business angle, having the FCC mandate a proprietary system is unprecedented. All previous systems for anything were all open source. The technology to create a piece of equipment was there, every parameter. With HD Radio, none of these parameters are public, at least not enough that some clever engineer could roll their own. This is very unfair, and smacks of a monopoly. The whole HD Radio specifications should have been in the public domain. Were someone to reverse-engineer this method, no doubt they would be hauled before a judge and significantly fined. All because some company has convinced the federal government that it has the only way to do the job. The parallel would be if the government decided that to drive on the interstate you had to buy a new Buick . . ."

Once again, the FCC is moving in a direction that will harm the consumer and limit the type and amount of information the public will receive, thereby limiting free speech. If the dire predictions come true and local AM radio bites the dust because of the IBOC digital broadcast scheme, what program types will be lost? The local AM stations are home to local news, sports, and information; ethnic programs; talk shows; Christian preaching and teaching; and other programs considered for "minority" tastes. Perhaps that includes programs that you listen to on your local AM radio station.

The problems with the AM digital transmission scheme will also prevent the old-fashioned broadcasting response to fires, floods, hurricanes, tornadoes, terrorism, and all sorts of catastrophes. The reason is that the so-called "clear channel" AM stations operating with 50kw of power at night will be silenced by the limitations of digital technology or will have gone off the air altogether. The interference and other problems encountered with this poorly conceived and poorly engineered system approved by FCC bureaucrats—who have no understanding of AM signals—will doom the very broadcasters who keep our nation informed.

Many contend that the FCC is simply incompetent when it comes to matters of broadcast technology. I cannot judge their competence, but I can say that these technology issues harm the free flow of information.

CHAPTER

4

The "Fairness Doctrine"

- History -

The policy of the Federal Communications Commission that was known as the "Fairness Doctrine" was promoted as an attempt to ensure that all coverage of controversial issues by a broadcast station be balanced and fair. The "Fairness Doctrine" was established by the FCC in 1949 and was abolished by it in 1987 during the Reagan Administration.

In 1949, when the FCC established the "Fairness Doctrine," the argument was that those who wanted to have licenses for broadcast stations were to act as "public trustees" of the airwaves. The basic premise has been that all airwaves (broadcast frequencies) belong to the public, and that the number of frequencies and licenses are few; therefore, anyone who is granted permission to use these frequencies has an obligation to guard the use of the airwaves for the public good.

The FCC used the "public trustee" concept to create an obligation of any licensee to provide reasonable opportunity for discussion of contrasting points of view on controversial issues of public importance. The Commission later held that stations were also obligated to actively seek out issues of importance to their community and air programming that addressed those issues. Officially, regulators were concerned that the burgeoning power of radio, and the infant medium of television following World War II should be harnessed to provide points of view from all perspectives. There were many applicants for relatively few licenses, and the FCC took the position that it would be a harm to the public for licensees to be advocates with a singular perspective. Broadcast licensees would be mandated by the FCC to make all voices heard.

The "Fairness Doctrine" eventually required much paperwork to please the FCC bureaucrats. The FCC went further into the content of programming with requirements concerning editorials aired on stations, political speech, perceived community needs, and more burdens on the broadcast licensees.

In fact, the "Fairness Doctrine" was an attempt to extend the reach of the FCC into the programming heard on the airwaves. Section 315 of the Communications Act of 1937 required stations to offer "equal opportunity" to all legally qualified political candidates for any office if they had allowed any person running in that office to use the station. However, this section of broadcast law exempted news programs, interviews and documentaries, whereas The "Fairness Doctrine" included such programs.

Although the "Fairness Doctrine" was not law, but simply FCC policy, it was used with powerful effect. In the 1969 "Red Lion" case, the United States Supreme Court ruled against Red Lion Broadcasting and upheld the "Fairness Doctrine." (See Appendix I for a first-hand report on the persecution caused by the "Fairness Doctrine.")

When the "Fairness Doctrine" was abolished in 1987, the FCC stated:

> "We no longer believe that the Fairness Doctrine, as a matter of policy, serves the public interests. In making this determination, we do not question the interest of the listening and viewing public in obtaining access to diverse and antagonistic sources of information. Rather, we conclude that the Fairness Doctrine is no longer a necessary or appropriate means by which to effectuate this interest. We believe that the interest of the public in viewpoint diversity is fully served by the multiplicity of voices in the marketplace today and that the intrusion by government into the content of programming occasioned by the enforcement of the doctrine unnecessarily restricts the journalistic freedom of broadcasters. Furthermore, we find that the Fairness Doctrine, in operation, actually inhibits the presentation of controversial issues of public importance to the detriment of the public and in degradation of the editorial prerogative of broadcast journalists."

If all one seeks is fairness—that is, relative equality of ideas—what is wrong with a policy of the regulatory agency that oversees broadcasters requiring such "fairness"?

Read on.

CHAPTER

5

The "Fairness Doctrine"

- Reality -

The policy of the FCC known as the "Fairness Doctrine" was conceived by President Harry Truman and his minions. Truman was fearful of an informed public and was especially fearful of the growing power of radio preachers in the political arena. He wanted to make sure that broadcasters would be careful not to allow anyone, including preachers, to have the only voice on an issue. That was accomplished by silencing free speech, hence the so-called "Fairness Doctrine."

The "Fairness Doctrine" was established by the FCC under Chairman Frieda Barkin Hennock, appointed by Harry Truman as the first female Chair of the Commission. Ms. Hennock was a native of Poland and had immigrated to New York where she received her legal training and practiced law. She had no background in broadcasting, communications, regulation, or anything to qualify her for the position.

The Museum of Broadcast Communications (http://www.museum.tv) has a biography of Hennock written by Lucy A. Liggett. In part, Ms. Liggett writes, "Before her nomination to serve on the FCC, Hennock had been practicing law in New York City. She had, as she told the Senate Committee during her confirmation hearings, no experience in broadcasting other than using radio to raise money for the political campaigns of Franklin Delano Roosevelt and other Democratic candidates . . . Hennock became convinced that television had the power to serve as an important educational tool. As the proposed table of television channel assignments was developed . . . Hennock was determined that the opportunity to use television for educating the audience not be lost. She . . . became an outspoken advocate for channel set-asides."

Ms. Hennock is acknowledged as the "Mother" of "educational television" and what has become PBS, the Public Broadcasting System.

There are those who would deny that PBS is educational. They see it as "edu-tainment" or "indoctrination." It depends on your viewpoint. The left-leaning programming of PBS has been documented. PBS and its government-funded television stations were never held accountable under the former "Fairness Doctrine." Without question, education is a good idea. But covering attempts at political indoctrination under the guise of education is not so good.

This denial of free speech to broadcasters by the "Fairness Doctrine" disturbed journalists who were free, in the print media, to say what they pleased without recourse. This author remembers working under the "Fairness Doctrine" and the chilling effect it had on everything scripted for use on each broadcast. Licensees were always on guard to protect their investment, careful not to cause any "ripple" in the airwaves by their news or other programs.

There were three stations that lost or surrendered their licenses when challenged by the FCC using the "Fairness Doctrine." Red Lion Broadcasting Company in the "Red Lion" case fought all the way to the U. S. Supreme Court, only to lose everything. The other two gave up in the midst of their battles.

Red Lion Broadcasting Company (WGCB – Word of God, Christ, Bible) lost its license because of one mention on a 15-minute, paid preaching broadcast that did not offer free time to an author whose book and person had been criticized. The cost of the time for the 15-minute broadcast was only $ 7.50. It was the principle of the guarantee of free speech that was at stake, not the money. Free speech lost the skirmish.

From the Supreme Court ruling we read:

> "The Red Lion Broadcasting Company is licensed to operate a Pennsylvania radio station, WGCB. On November 27, 1964, WGCB carried a 15-minute broadcast by the Reverend Billy James Hargis as part of a "Christian Crusade" series. A book by Fred J. Cook entitled "Goldwater - Extremist on the Right" was discussed by Hargis, who said that Cook had been fired by a newspaper for making false charges against city officials; that Cook had then worked for a Communist-affiliated publication; that he had defended Alger Hiss and attacked J. Edgar Hoover and the Central Intelligence Agency; and that he had now

written a "book to smear and destroy Barry Goldwater."[note 2] When Cook heard of the broadcast he [372] concluded that he had been personally attacked and demanded free reply time, which the station refused. After an exchange of letters among Cook, Red Lion, and the FCC, the FCC declared that the Hargis broadcast constituted a personal attack on Cook; that Red Lion had failed to meet its obligation under the fairness doctrine as expressed in Times-Mirror Broadcasting Co., 24 P & F Radio Reg. 404 (1962), to send a tape, transcript, or summary of the broadcast to Cook and offer him reply time; and that the station must provide reply time whether or not Cook would pay for it. On review in the Court of Appeals for the District of Columbia Circuit,[note 3] the [373] FCC's position was upheld as constitutional and otherwise proper. 127 U.S. App. D.C. 129, 381 F.2d 908 (1967)."

You might want to know that Mr. Cook was accused by the former President of CBS News, Fred W. Friendly, of taking action against WGCB radio as part of the orchestrated plot of the Democrat National Committee and the administration of President Lyndon Johnson. Mr. Cook denied the accusation.

In his book, *The Good Guys, the Bad Guys, and the First Amendment*, published in 1976, Friendly quoted a former Kennedy official and public relations consultant for the Johnson presidential campaign, Bill Ruder, as saying "Our massive strategy was to use the Fairness Doctrine to challenge and harass right-wing broadcasters and hope the challenges would be so costly to them that they would be inhibited and decide it was too expensive to continue."

According to Friendly's book, the Democratic National Committee understood that conservatives operated on a cash basis and used a number of small, rural, radio stations who had low charges for broadcasts. A Democrat operative was quoted as saying, "Were our efforts to be continued on a year-round basis, we would find that many of these stations would consider the broadcasts of these programs bothersome and burdensome (especially if they are ultimately required to give us free time) and would start dropping the programs from their broadcast schedule." Friendly wrote that [the operative] said, "Perhaps in the light of Watergate, our tactics were too aggressive, but we were up against ultra-right preachers who were saying vicious things about Kennedy and Johnson."

The Republicans have also been guilty of trying to stifle free speech. When Nixon took office in 1969, he used the "Fairness Doctrine" as a weapon. Republican activists were recruited to file challenges against broadcast stations by using the "Fairness Doctrine" when the stations broadcast statements negative to the Administration or [that] the Vietnam War was considered to be unfair.

Although many challenges were filed against broadcasters by those elitists who fear the truth, only three such challenges resulted in the loss of station licenses. Why these three radio stations? Were these stations promoting some liberal agenda? Were they calling for revolution? Were they protesting against some government action or policy? Were they spreading lies?

No.

Each of these radio stations was a facility that aired programs of Christian and patriotic themes. Their programs aired views of truth, goodness, virtue, life, observance of morality, obedience to the laws of the land, and patriotic valor.

They were targeted by the left-wing radicals of their time because they stood for godly government. The elitist bureaucracy pursued the challenges against them. They were targeted, attacked, and deprived of their licenses and their voices.

As we put the "reality" puzzle together, we must add some evidence to my statement concerning Harry Truman and his fear of "Gospel Preachers." It is my contention that it was the Government's fear of the preaching of the Gospel that birthed the "Fairness Doctrine." Please read on, and I believe you will understand why I make this statement.

6

Courageous Pastor and Broadcast Pioneer: Dr. J. Harold Smith

D r. J. Harold Smith was a Pastor who had a broadcast on radio station WNOX in Knoxville, Tennessee, in the 1940s. In 1946, WNOX decided to pull all paid religious broadcasts. This was a move that was repeated many times across the country as the Federal Council of Churches (now the National Council of Churches) flexed their political muscle to keep fundamentalist Christian programs off the air (see Appendix IV, The NCC).

J. Harold Smith, 1936

Liberal churchmen have never learned the lesson that liberal theology is never popular if the public is given the choice between the fundamentalist (conservatives) and mainline (liberals). We see it today, not only in the church world, but also in the talk show realm.

Pastor Smith led a great protest march in April 1946 that made the newspapers all over the country. He later discussed the events in a 1995 interview from his Radio Bible Hour studios with his son, Donald Smith. Dr. Smith explained:

But [by leading the march] I created three powerful enemies, son. First of all was the liquor crowd. I really had that crowd breathing down my neck. The next was the National Council, or Federal Council as it was known then, of Churches in America—the liberal element of the church. And the third group were the Communists. And I mean—in 1937, '38, '39, '40, '41, and '42—it's unbelievable how the Communists were in this country and how they had infiltrated many of our places.

In the early 40s, I moved the ministry to Knoxville and we were on one of the great stations over there. We had been on that station three or four years when the National Council of Churches moved in—and in one week they put 1100 churches and preachers across America off the radio. And the only ones that could be on radio would be the ones that would come to the National Council of Churches or the Federal Council of Churches.

Well, we put on a protest in Knoxville. And up until that time, there had never been a crowd—not even to a Vols [University of Tennessee Volunteers] football game—of 50,000 people. Our enemy paper there (Knoxville *News-Sentinel*) estimated that we had 35,000 people. But the *Journal*, our friend paper there, estimated we had over 50,000—the largest crowd up until that time that had ever assembled in one group in Knoxville, Tennessee.

We marched down the street and stopped right in front of the *News-Sentinel* and protested. And I preached. Well, they boarded up WNOX—they thought we were going to tear up the place. I never had in mind of hurting a flea, you know. I wasn't going to burn no buildings. I wasn't going to shoot nobody. Never had that in mind. I just wanted to tell 'em I didn't agree with 'em. And I still believe that I have a right to do it.

I don't believe in bombing buildings like they did in Oklahoma City. I believe that's wrong. I don't believe, I tell you, in assassinating people like they did Martin Luther King. Like they did John Kennedy and his brother. I don't believe in that. I believe that if you don't like what goes on politically, you ought to change it by a ballot and not by a bullet. That's always been my philosophy.

So we applied for a radio station. And the FCC granted it. They didn't know who they was giving it to. But when we put on that parade, that news got to Washington. It got the attention of President Truman and President Truman said *we have got to stop that bird. Boy, he's getting too much power down there in the state of Tennessee, and the next thing you know he'll be another Huey Long in Louisiana!*
And so, we went on the air on the eleventh day of July in 1944.

And the next month, in came the FCC. And for about six years we fought them all the way to the Supreme Court of the United States of America. And they claimed that I owned XERF, or a part of XERF, on the [Mexican] border because of our investment that we made down there in about 1945.

J. Harold Smith
Behind the Microphone, 1941

And in that investment, I bought air time. I bought from 6:00 in the morning 'til 6:30, and from 8 'til 8:30 at night. And we paid $100,000 for that time. But in order to protect myself across the border in Mexico, we had to have a firm of lawyers to draw up the papers that they could not sell the station without my permission. If they did sell it, they had to give me a third of the sale price of it.

And the Supreme Court of the United States ruled that I owned a third of the stock of that station. And, Son, we brought Mr. Arturo Gonzales to Knoxville. He sat on the witness stand and testified—he's an attorney. He's still alive today and he's my friend to this very day. And he sat there and said, "Reverend Smith owns no part of XERF." But they ruled [on] it, and when the committee left Washington to come to Knoxville for the trial, they had orders from the White House that they were not to come back unless they had our license for that station.

And so, we just went through hell on this earth. I mean they told every sort of a lie. They said I had $400,000 in the bank. And that was all the time we were there...all these years, all the money we'd ever deposited in the Park National Bank...for all those years. And they said, he's got $400,000. And when they printed that in headlines in the enemy paper there in Knoxville, I had less than $500 in the bank!

And I am so blessed. We were the first in radio, then we were the first almost in television. I think that I'm the first person that ever spoke a Scripture on television. Your mother and I were in New York City in 1935. And we were making a tour of the RCA building. And the guide said, "on the 35th floor, we are experimenting with a thing called television." And he said, "if any of you would like to speak, and let the others go in the next room and hear you, why, do it."

I put up my hand. I went in and they put me before that camera... and Mother and all of them were in the other room, and I quoted John 3:16 on that station. So, long before there was ever a radio station in this part of the country, long before we have TV, long before there was ever a set made...while I was in there experimenting...I believe I'm the first person that ever quoted a Scripture verse on television.

And then we were one of the first, you know, to ever have a program right from the auditorium of our church. And that started in 1953 in Fort Smith, Arkansas, and I took that program and we were the first to come on the air. That program is still going from the First Baptist Church in Fort Smith, Arkansas, to this very minute. So it's the longest Sunday auditorium religious television broadcast....

There's a lot of history, real history, back in my life, you know.

What happened to Dr. Smith happened before the "Fairness Doctrine." His success with the masses helped cause the government to enact the "Fairness Doctrine." If this odious denial of free speech is resurrected, what will happen to the Truth and those who tell it?

CHAPTER

7

"Termites in the Temple"

J. Harold Smith In the Pulpit

Portions of a Sermon Preached To 30,000 People
At a Protest Meeting
On Sunday, April 14, 1946, Knoxville, Tennessee
By Rev. J. Harold Smith
(Abridged Version)
See Appendix III for the full text of the speech

It has been no easy thing to wrestle against powers, against the rulers of the darkness of this world, against spiritual wickedness in high places.

But we feel that we have a cause, a right, a privilege and a glorious freedom at stake. Our liberties are more valuable than life itself. Did our boys not gladly go into the withering machine gun fire at Okinawa, did they not march over the dead bodies of their buddies on the beachhead of Normandy, that we might enjoy the liberties that spell America and not Russia?

The Text

Our text is found in the Old Testament in the Book of Ezekiel, chapter 8, verse 7:

> "And he brought me to the door of the court;
> and when I looked, behold a hole in the wall."

> Then verse 8 declares, "Then said he
> unto me, 'Son of man, dig now in the wall': and
> when I had digged in the wall, behold a door.

> Verse 9: "And he said unto me, 'Go in and
> behold the wicked abominations that they
> do here.'"

> Verse 10, "And so I went in and

> saw; and behold every form of creeping
> things and abominable hearts, and all the
> idols of the house of Israel, portrayed upon
> the wall round about."

God's man was allowed to see on the inside. Ezekiel saw the abominations that were working on the inside; and my friends, I declare we need to see the things underneath these strange movements that are now progressing. By the grace of God, I want you to take a peep this afternoon through the "hole in the wall" and see "the wicked abominations that they do here."

Principle Involved

You came here because of a principle—a right that you believe in, that I believe in, that every true American believes in—and that is Right and Justice for all—regardless of whether he be Jew, or Greek, white or black, weak or strong, rich or poor.

If this struggle only involved the few so-called "Racketeering Radio Preachers," I would not waste my time in protesting. I would not have begged you to come to this central meeting place. My friends, I have called you here that we might get a look through the "Hole in the wall" at the "Abominations that they do here."

I am shocked, yea, even amazed that so soon—even before scores of our returning veterans have found a job or their gaping wounds healed—an attempt [is being] made to take away from us one of the four freedoms that the late President, Franklin D. Roosevelt, so faithfully assured us would be our heritage and that of our children—if we would only sacrifice our husbands and sons and fathers and sweethearts on the battle fields of Europe and the hot steaming jungles of the far away Pacific.

Was he only kidding us? From the recent action taken by "your *News-Sentinel* Station, WNOX," one would judge that there will have to be another battle for you G.I.'s to fight!

There was a time before the war when your Knoxville *News-Sentinel* Station WNOX was very anxious to sell preachers [air] time. Then, she had NO convictions about taking [money] away from "poor preachers." Not until two weeks ago did they have this change of heart. They said they had been convicted in this matter--that their conscience hurt them over selling time to preachers. Well, they haven't said anything about giving all the money I have paid them the past five years back to me! If they did it would be to the tune of about $60,000. I am not complaining about the money I have paid the station. I do not regret it. Just one soul of the thousands who have been saved as a result of this broadcast and of the other preachers who have so faithfully declared God's Word is worth every dollar spent and every tear shed, and every hour of preparing the messages. Just to visit every day in the home of cripples, of the aged, of the invalid, of the sinner and the saint by radio was worth it all. My stay in Knoxville and my broadcasting over the "*News-Sentinel*" Station WNOX has been a most pleasant one.

WNOX Grows Rich

I repeat: there was a time before the war when WNOX was in her infancy, when she was little and weak. She needed financial support. The preachers were welcome then with their "shekels," but now your *News-Sentinel* Station WNOX has grown into a mighty giant. She is East Tennessee's most powerful radio station. She has grown rich. Last year, she did over $500,000—one-half million dollars' worth of business. I repeat: "your *News-Sentinel* Station WNOX" has grown rich off the "blood of your sons." Big business, beer and cigarettes prospered during the war. They were able to buy more time. That's all right, too. They have the right to buy it if they have the money, *and so do I!*

Your *News-Sentinel* Station WNOX has been blessed. The Bible says that God blessed Pharaoh for Joseph, his servant's sake. Your *News-Sentinel* Station WNOX, up until two weeks ago, was friendly toward the Gospel. They sold to all alike. But orders came down from an "absentee owner" who lives in New York City, saying "Get all those "Hill-Billy" preachers off my *News-Sentinel* Station WNOX by April

15th. I had thought up until then it was *"your"* News-Sentinel Station," but now I have learned that it is Mr. Jack Howard's, of 230 Park Avenue, New York City, New York. They say they have to "ban" us preachers. That's right! They haven't banned us, they have "canned" us.

"All Can Advertise"

Yes, friends, every one can advertise over the *News-Sentinel* Station, WNOX—[everyone] but preachers. Why, they advertise ice cream, cigarettes and candy. They advertise chewing gum, furniture, automobiles, soft drinks, headache pills, and "Rooster Snuff." They sell time to *Life Magazine, True story, Saturday Evening Post,* and ever so often you hear them put in one of these little "ditties":

> "Tick-Tock, Ten o'clock,
> Tick-Tock, Two o'clock,
> Tic-Tock, Four o'clock,
> Time to stop and get a cold 'Doc'
> When you're hungry, thirsty and tired."

Or, maybe it's:

> "Pepsi-Cola hits the spot,
> Twelve full ounces that's a lot,
> Twice as much for a nickel too,
> Pepsi-Cola is the drink for you."

Now, friends, I have nothing against these companies. Right now, in fact, a good Pepsi would be O.K.; and as thirsty as I am, a Dr. Pepper would hit the spot. But if all these things can come over your radio, why should I be kept from saying, "For God so loved the world that He gave His only begotten Son, that whosoever believeth on Him should not perish but have everlasting life"?

I have yet to be shown I don't have that right. Someone beside Mr. Jack Howard, owner of the *News-Sentinel* Station will have to tell me I don't have that right before I will believe it.

I further contend that if the program I put on the air is one that serves the "public interest, convenience, and necessity" then I have a right to be heard. Mr. Jack Howard, neither the Knoxville *News-Sentinel* [nor] WNOX owns the air waves. They belong to the people, and are only loaned by our government [to Mr. Howard]. If he misuses them, then they may be taken away. It would indeed be said, should the people of this section rise up in such a mighty and indignant protest, that F.C.C. should take away the license of said station. It is not at all impossible for such a thing to be done.

"Price Tags"

Our beloved editor of the Knoxville *News-Sentinel* goes on to say (quote), "in effect, the decision removed the "price tag" from religion" (end quote). Well, since when did this said editor become so interested in "price tags"? We have never argued with the Station officials at WNOX about the "price tags." You, friends, who for five years have never failed to support these religious programs, have never worried about these "price tags." Maybe it is the Editor's "high blood pressure" that is causing him to worry about these "price tags." I don't know the editor of the *News-Sentinel*, writer of "No Price On Religion," but I am sure I could take twenty-five cents and pay him off in full for all he has ever donated to any religious program that had for its purpose the winning of lost souls to God. Those who always holler about the "cost" and the "money" of said programs are generally the tight wads, skin-flints, nickel nibblers, and penny-pinchers of your community. You're welcome!

He further states (quote), "We suppose this policy has long been in effect elsewhere in the country, and that it has the approval of the Federal Communications Commission" (end quote). Yes, I am sorry to add that "this policy" has "long been" in effect—in countries [such as] Italy, Japan, Germany, and Russia. Every radio station that Scripps-Howard, Inc, gets their hands on soon falls under the axe. Believe my friends, when I tell you that the Termite of Communism is gnawing the "mud-sills" of our Christian foundations from beneath us. If we are to attach importance to latest reports, Russia is definitely out to conquer the world.

Do you know the one thing that stands in Moscow's way more than anything else? I will tell you: *It is the Children of God*, regardless of denominational affiliations or race. God's saints stand as the great force opposing this termite. Communism is anti-God, anti-Christ, and anti-Church. Christians are pro-God, pro-Christ, pro-Church. Joseph Stalin knows that the loyal followers of Christ must be silenced in America in order to "put over" his program.

I am in receipt of a letter from a dear brother preacher, Rev. D.B Eastep, Pastor of Calvary Baptist Church in Covington, Kentucky, dated April 5, 1946. I quote from the letter: "This letter is to inform you that after six years of broadcasting over WCTO at Cincinnati, Ohio, we have been taken off this station. This is not the cause of any preference of ours. We believe that it is directly or indirectly the cause of the Federal Council of Churches." Friends, this is another termite in the temple. This termite is as filthy as the first, Communism. Brother Eastep went on to say, "The time which we and other fundamental churches used and paid for over this station is now being given free to three 'representative' groups, one of which is the Federal Council of Churches. Ask your pastor: Does *his* church belong to the Federal Council? And if it does, get out of that church—*fast*. Flee it like you would a den of rattlesnakes! This organization is from Hell! It is a wolf in sheep's clothing. It is a green-eyed monster devouring the faith. I repeat: the Federal Council of Churches is from Hell!

Rules Of Life

I tell you, WNOX and the *News-Sentinel* are these days being taught the rules of life. They have much to learn about Americanism, about the power of prayer. I wouldn't have all the prayers going up against *me* that are going up against WNOX and this godless newspaper that has no respect for sobriety, but would make drunkards out of your sons and prostitutes out of your daughters, with her open declaration against God's Holy law "of keeping the Sabbath day Holy"—and in her hellish efforts to bring to our fair city the cursed "Liquor Store." I have been living in Knoxville five years and didn't know until recently that our city was infested with "gangsters" until certain people began to recognize them on our city streets. How did they know them? [Explanatory Note: "Gangsters" was the derogatory term used by the Knoxville *News-Sentinel* to describe preachers of the Gospel such as Dr. Smith.]

Yes, I repeat: WNOX and the Knoxville *News-Sentinel* need to learn about the precision and efficiency with which Christians operate when stirred—about the attitudes of Americans in East Tennessee, the Old Volunteer State, where men are men. Yes, I repeat: about their attitudes toward atheistic, alien, anti-Christ, anti-Bible, anti-Church Communism.

I charge that in this "new policy" adopted by WNOX they are striking a death blow to one of the most blessed of our freedoms—that of worshipping God according to the dictates of our own hearts—and [the right] of free speech. I charge that this "new policy" puts every advertiser at the mercy of these would-be dictators. Someone has said, "Give the Devil enough rope and he will hang himself." I believe if WNOX insists on keeping in force her "New Policy," and the *News-Sentinel* continues its anti-God, anti-Church, anti-Bible, and anti-preacher attacks, that we are witnessing a "double hanging" here this afternoon!

Think of the broken homes, broken lives, broken hearts, liquor has caused. Think of the sad-eyed mothers, the pale, sick, nervous wives liquor has caused. Think of the little hungry, orphaned children liquor has caused. I want to go on record before all of you as being against liquor—whether it is bootlegged or sold in a legalized liquor store. I want to go on record as being on the opposite side of those who advocate its sale and advertise its products.

Conclusion

Our boys fought, they waded through Hell on earth, they gave up home and loved ones that this American privilege might be ours. I declare that by the grace of God, the *News-Sentinel* and WNOX shall not destroy these blessed principles.

I pray that by the grace of God this "New Policy" may not prevail, but may His Word prevail and the cause of Christ this day march on to one of the greatest Christian victories of our generation.

We will now form in our parade march on WNOX. This parade, I am sure, will be in the Spirit of Christ. I know it will be orderly, and any misconduct will count only for our enemy. This march will be for the glory of God. When we reach the station, there will be a prayer and then our parade will proceed to the old "Mother Bear's Den," The Knoxville *News-Sentinel*. WNOX is only the "Little Cub Bear." Another prayer, and you will be dismissed. As you march, pray.

CHAPTER

8

Attempts to
Deny Free Speech

Since the abolition of the "Fairness Doctrine" in 1987, Congressional Democrats have introduced legislation to re-instate it. Actually, these proposed laws would go further by basing the rule of "fairness" in law, not as simply a rule of the bureaucrats.

In the spring of 1987, both houses of Congress voted to put the "Fairness Doctrine" into law, making it enforceable by the Federal Communications Commission. President Reagan vetoed the legislation, and there were insufficient votes to override the veto.

In 1988, in a speech to the National Association of Broadcasters, President Reagan remarked, "As you know, I've never liked big government. And that was one of the reasons I was opposed to the so-called Fairness Doctrine, as you've already been told—that particular legislation which I vetoed. And I think you'll agree, there's no reason to substitute the judgment of Washington bureaucrats for that of professional broadcasters."

The good news is that a resurrected "Fairness Doctrine" has not seen the light of day. All attempts since the Spring of 1987 have ended in failure. In June of 2007, the House voted overwhelmingly (309-115) to prohibit the FCC from using taxpayer dollars to impose the "Fairness Doctrine" on broadcasters. This was a pre-emptive strike by Republicans who were worried about the possible new "Fairness Doctrine" should the Democrats win the Presidency in 2008.

In an article by Alexander Bolton in the June 28, 2007, edition of "The Hill," it was reported:

> "Senate Majority Whip Dick Durbin (D-Ill.) said on Tuesday that the government should revive the Fairness Doctrine…that required broadcasters to balance political content with different points of view.

> "'It's time to re-institute the Fairness Doctrine,' he said. 'I have this old-fashioned attitude that when Americans hear both sides

of the story, they're in a better position to make a decision.'

"Sen. Dianne Feinstein (D-California.), chairwoman of the Senate Rules Committee, said . . . that she would review the constitutional and legal issues involved in re-establishing the doctrine.

"Sen. John Kerry (Mass.), the Democratic Party's 2004 presidential nominee, also said recently that the Fairness Doctrine should return."

The amendment was sponsored by Indiana Republican Representative Mike Pence, himself a former talk show host, who said before the vote, "This House will say what some in the other body are not saying, that we believe in freedom on the airwaves. We reject the doctrines of the past that would have this federal government manage political speech on the public airwaves."

Other Republicans joined with Pence to shut off any funding. The House Minority Leader, John Boehner (R-Ohio) was quoted as saying, "The best way is to let the judgment of the American people decide, and they can decide with their finger. (They) can turn it off or they can turn it on. They can go to their computer and read it on the Internet."

Following the vote, Republican Whip Roy Blunt authored a column on the Fairness Doctrine in the *Springfield* (Missouri) *News-Leader*. He wrote:

"...The provision ended up cruising through with more than 300 members in support. But though the final tally was overwhelming, the fact we didn't get the entire chamber on our side reminds us that, at least among 115 members of the House and more than a few members of the Senate, the restoration of the un-fairness doctrine isn't only a serious possibility — it's a real priority.

"Thankfully, the latest attempt to resurrect the doctrine didn't need a ruling from the Supreme Court or a veto from the president to be brought to heel. But that's not to say they won't be needed in the future, especially as powerful interests line up with the objective of having government regulators control the content of opinion and the terms of public debate."

The trade associations and those involved in broadcasting realize the threat. This is from a letter to the author dated December 21, 2007, from David K. Rehr, President and CEO of the National Association of Broadcasters. He writes:

"NAB continued to wage the battle against reinstatement of the Fairness Doctrine. NAB supported the effort in the House of Representatives to preclude the FCC from using its resources to reinstate the outdated policy. The amendment passed the House of Representatives by a vote of 309 – 115. Additionally, the final omnibus appropriations bill, which is being considered by Congress as you read this letter, may also include language to prohibit reinstatement. NAB will continue to stave off any attempts to reinstate the Fairness Doctrine."

This was received from the Virginia Association of Broadcasters in July of 2007:

"Senators Diane Feinstein (D-CA) and Dick Durbin (D-IL) made headlines last month when they endorsed the revival of the Fairness Doctrine, a regulatory relic that required broadcasters to ensure balanced coverage of opposing viewpoints when reporting on controversial issues. Federal appellate courts called the doctrine into question in the 1980s, and the FCC later repealed its Fairness Doctrine regulations.

"Shortly after Senators Feinstein and Durbin made headlines, several Republican members of the Congress in the House offered an amendment to an appropriations bill to prevent the

FCC from spending any funds to implement or otherwise enforce the Fairness Doctrine (even if the doctrine were somehow revived). The amendment passed and was approved by the full House. Congressman Mike Pence (R-IN) also introduced a bill in the House (H.R. 2905) and Senators John Thune (R-SD) and Norm Coleman (R-MN) introduced separate bills in the Senate (S. 1742, S. 1748) that would prevent the FCC from re-promulgating the Fairness Doctrine.

"Feinstein's and Durbin's endorsement is just the most recent in several attempts since the late 1980s to give the Fairness Doctrine new life. Although Democratic House headers claimed they had no plan to revive the doctrine and dismissed the Republican-introduced appropriations amendment as a 'political stunt,' the issue may not be dead yet. It is still possible that the House Commerce Committee could hold hearings on various proposals to reintroduce 'fairness' into the media's presentation of political issues, and Senate Republicans are actively seeking a vote on Senator Coleman's proposal to prevent the FCC from reinstating the doctrine. Indeed, the current debate regarding a Fairness Doctrine revival indicates that broadcast programming, and perhaps public affairs and political programming in particular, are rising to the top of legislative agendas. These are issues to watch as we approach the upcoming national election season."

The good news is that America and its broadcasters do not have the intrusion of the "Fairness Doctrine" in their programming. The bad news is that the Democrats are continuing to lead the charge for the re-institution of the "Fairness Doctrine." Not only do they want it re-instituted, they hope to enlarge the scope of the regulation.

A senior research fellow in regulatory policy at the Heritage Foundation, James L. Gattuso, writes that the Democrats have decided to implement a new strategy, perhaps not moving toward the "Fairness Doctrine" too quickly. His article was posted at www.heritage.org. He writes that the

Democrats plan to work toward the following:

- Strengthened limits on how many radio stations one firm can own, locally and nationally;
- Shortening broadcast license terms;
- Requiring radio broadcasters to regularly show they are operating in the "public interest;" and
- Imposing a fee on broadcasters who fail to meet these "public interest obligations," with the funding to go to the Corporation for Public Broadcasting.

Gatusso also reports, "The goal of the reforms is the same as the Fairness Doctrine: to reduce the influence of conservative talk radio. Limiting ownership, the authors believe, will eliminate many of the owners who favor conservative causes. Public interest requirements can be defined almost any way a regulator wants—up to and perhaps even beyond that required by the old Fairness Doctrine. And the proposed fee provides regulators with a quite effective stick to compel compliance—as well as to direct funds to more ideologically compatible public broadcasters.

"Free speech and free markets enjoyed a great victory last week in the defeat of the Fairness Doctrine. But the real fight to protect the media from government interference is just beginning."

When you add the specter of hate speech laws (proposed by Democrats after the Canadian model) to the prospects of a renewed "Fairness Doctrine," it is starkly apparent that we must not let our guard down.

Be ever vigilant.

CHAPTER

9

What If the "Fairness Doctrine" Were Resurrected?

If the "Fairness Doctrine" were once again the rule by which broadcasters were forced to operate, there would be little or no talk radio, as we know it today. The one person who is arguably most responsible for modern talk radio, Rush Limbaugh, could not have begun the modern talk radio genre until 1988, the year after the elimination of the "Fairness Doctrine."

Not only would talk radio be eliminated, but radio and television stations that broadcast Christian teaching would be under siege. Imagine a minister of the Gospel quoting Christ Jesus from John 14:6: *"Jesus saith unto him, I am the way, the truth, and the life: no man cometh unto the Father, but by me."* Any of the rest of Scripture as it pertains to life, sin, relationships, salvation, and eternity would be prohibited, and Christian talk and teaching stations would be a thing of the past.

Think of your favorite Christian music radio station. How much of its music is now instrumental only—without lyrics? If the "Fairness Doctrine" were to be reinstated, we would have to get used to hearing instrumental music only, lest someone be "offended" by the Christian message contained in the lyrics and complain, using the new "Fairness Doctrine" as a weapon against the station.

The Chairman of Salem Communications Corporation, Stuart Epperson, on August 23, 2007 wrote:

"If the Fairness Doctrine is reinstated, history indicates these things (and more) will happen:

1. The First Amendment, which these days seems to be the number one target, will again be significantly depreciated, further eroding our Freedom of Speech.

2. The political party in power will use the Fairness Doctrine to silence critics, as was well documented during the Kennedy and Nixon administrations.

3. Many leading Broadcast Licensees will see their licenses at risk and will play it safe by imposing strict speech control.

4. The national and local robust town hall meetings known as Talk Radio will quickly become mundane, dull and milk-toast-like and mostly disappear.

5. Religious speech will be threatened by new government guidelines regarding what constitutes controversial and public issues... issues like same-sex marriage and abortion.

6. The overwhelming majority of the time the public will hear only the Liberal viewpoint, presented as "fair and balanced" by the three major TV Networks, the vast majority of newspapers, and the major magazines. *Déjà vu!*"

Epperson's Conclusion: "The Fairness Doctrine's frontal assault on Freedom of Speech not only trashes a vital part of our Constitution but does great harm to our country, nationally and locally by stopping a healthy public debate that is essential in our common search for TRUTH."

Even the *Los Angeles Times* understands the potential, as evidenced by an editorial in that publication on July 31, 2007, under the title "The Unfairness Doctrine":

"...The threat to talk radio is clear. If the rule were re-instituted, stations that carry Rush Limbaugh could be forced to broadcast commentaries favoring everything that Limbaugh derides, from greenhouse gas controls to same-sex marriage. With hundreds of provocative talk-show hosts on the air, federal regulators could soon be awash in demands for rebuttals.

"But the danger posed by the Fairness Doctrine is broader and more fundamental than an attack on a radio format. No matter what your point of view might be, you have free or inexpensive outlets available today to express them—maybe not a radio or TV station but certainly a website, a video blog, a pod-cast or an e-mail newsletter. At the same time, the public has unprecedented access to a diverse array of opinions. Just as the government shouldn't decide what you say on the channels you create, [neither] should it be able to dictate the range of opinions people hear over the air..."

Over 4,000 Local, Over-the-air Stations Could Lose Their Licenses

Look at the numbers from Arbitron's Radio Today 2007 when you think of what would be lost if the "Fairness Doctrine" were to become the rule once more. The second most popular format in the country is News/Talk/Information, heard weekly by more than 47 million people and aired on 1,503 stations. When you add all the other news and talk formats, this type of informational programming is heard on 1,804 radio stations. Add to that the 2,203 radio stations broadcasting with a religious format and you have a total of 4,007 local over-the-air radio stations that could lose their licenses. Remember that 92.8% of all Americans listen to radio each week. It is no wonder that the Democrats are worried. If the truth really were acted upon, we would have a new leadership in our country.

If the Democrats were in complete control, having enacted "Hate Speech" laws and a new "Fairness Doctrine," what would keep them from shutting down stations and taking their licenses? It has happened in Canada and Venezuela. The European Union and its member states have quotas for various content in advertising and programming, with the threat of loss of license if the broadcaster is errant.

If the liberal Democrats have their way and the "Fairness Doctrine" is reinstated by the Federal Communications Commission or by Congress, expect the radio and television programs that tell the truth—about anything—to be gone. Expect only the liberal, leftist, humanist agenda to be presented as truth. Expect everything you believe in and stand for to be ridiculed and maligned, without recourse or rebuttal by the talk and Christian radio and television stations.

10

FLANK ATTACK:

One More Attempt to

Silence Broadcasters

The re-imposition of the "Fairness Doctrine" is the major effort of the liberals and elitists to silence the truth on the nation's airwaves. However, a related effort is revealed in the recent announcement by a well-known Republican Senator that he was seeking information about the financial dealings of six of today's "prosperity" televangelists. This produced a chilling effect on media ministries and on churches that use the electronic media to deliver their message.

In November of 2007, Senator Charles (Chuck) E. Grassley (R-Iowa), ranking member of the Senate Committee on Finance, issued letters initiating an investigation of six church/television ministries. The investigation did not cover any churches or ministries that were not involved in electronic communication. This could be a precursor to investigations and sanctions for other media organizations, as well. It may be used to "chill" the freedom of speech as well as damage the freedom of religion.

In a release from the Senate Finance Committee, Senator Grassley stated, "I'm following up on complaints from the public and news coverage regarding certain practices at six ministries. The allegations involve governing boards that aren't independent and [which] allow generous salaries and housing allowances and amenities such as private jets and Rolls Royces. I don't want to conclude that there's a problem, but I have an obligation to donors and the taxpayers to find out more. People who donated should have their money spent as intended and in adherence with the tax code."

Senator Grassley wrote to each of the six with the following introduction:

> "The [Senate] Finance Committee has a long tradition of reviewing tax-exempt organizations. It is important that the Congress and public have confidence that public charities, which benefit from very significant tax breaks, are operated in a manner that promotes continued trust and that these charities adhere to guidelines established by the Internal Revenue Service. Historically, Americans have given generously to

religious organizations, and those who do so should be assured that their donations are being used for the tax-exempt purposes of the organizations.

"Recent articles and news reports regarding the possible misuse of donations made to religious organizations have caused some concern for the Finance Committee. Since your organization is not required to file Form 990 with the Internal Revenue Service, we are requesting that you answer the following questions and provide the following information for our review.

"Please provide the requested information on searchable disks or electronically by December 6, 2007."

Senator Grassley's letters (available at www.finance.senate.gov) were then specific to each of the ministries, and included questions about payments, salaries, purchases, trips and other items of expense, including amenities given to the ministers in question. The Senator targeted Without Walls International Church/Randy & Paula White; World Healing Center Church, Inc./Benedictus (Benny) Hinn; New Birth Missionary Baptist Church/Eddie L. Long; World Changers Church International/Creflo and Taffi Dollar; Joyce Meyer Ministries/David & Joyce Meyer; and Kenneth Copeland Ministries/Kenneth Kenneth & Gloria Copeland.

Each of these ministries/ministers is known for a charismatic "prosperity gospel" and for their lifestyle based upon their teachings.

The Committee's press release concluded, "Grassley has reviewed a wide range of non-profit issues over the last five years, first as Finance Committee chairman and now as ranking member. The committee has exclusive Senate jurisdiction over federal tax policy, including the policy governing the billions of dollars donated to and controlled by the nation's tax-exempt groups."

In recent years, Senator Grassley has been known for his aggressive investigation of the Smithsonian Institution, the Nature Conservancy and the American Red Cross. Apparently the Senator is an equal opportunity investigator.

Senator Grassley is also known for his sponsorship of the Church Audit Procedures Act of 1983 that sought to balance the lawmaking interests of Congress with the rights of churches. According to the Internal Revenue Service, the law greatly expanded the statutory restrictions on the way the IRS handles inquiries and examinations of churches. The IRS states in its e-topics at <u>IRS.gov</u>: "Congress's actions were motivated by two competing considerations. First, Congress was aware of the special problems, including *problems of separation of church and state*, and *the special relationship of a church to its members* [italics added for clarification] that arise when the IRS (or any governmental agency) examines the records of a church . . ."

Read on.

CHAPTER

11

"Investigation" -
or "Inquisition"?

The *Tampa Tribune* website (www.tampatrib.com) featured the background questions and answers concerning the investigation by Senator Grassley that was the topic of the preceding chapter. The newspaper obtained the file from the Senate Finance Committee and made it available on the Internet. This is the "official" word concerning the process of the investigation:

Background Questions and Answers on Letters to Six Media-oriented Ministries from Sen. Chuck Grassley, Ranking Member, Senate Committee on Finance November 1, 2007

Q1. How did Sen. Grassley choose the six ministries that will receive his letters?

A1. Over the last few years there has been an increasing amount of disturbing news coverage regarding potential abuses by many ministries. Sen. Grassley, via his Finance Committee staff, chose the six ministries based on information provided to his staff by interested third parties, published news reports, and television news stories. Some of the accounts were disturbing because there continues to be a lack of transparency regarding how these ministries spend millions of dollars, and as an industry, billions of dollars that have been exempt from federal tax.

(One might ask, Why six and not twelve or three? Are "prosperity preachers" the only ones that "need" to be investigated or are they the first to be investigated?)

Q2. What will happen if the ministries don't give Sen. Grassley the information he's seeking?

A2. He expects full cooperation. It's very rare for him as ranking member of the committee, and chairman prior to becoming ranking member, not to get full cooperation with information requests.

Q3. What will happen if he receives the information he's seeking?

A3. Sen. Grassley's staff will review all of the documentation received and try to determine if there have been any abuses or possible violations of current tax law that should be referred to the appropriate enforcement agency. His committee staff also will consider whether any of the organizations have taken actions that may go against the spirit and intent of the law, and perhaps will consult with outside experts for advice. It's often the case that such investigations yield actions that are perfectly legal but shock the conscience and thereby highlight shortcomings in current law or in the enforcement of that law. But until the information is received and a review takes place, it's premature to say what future actions Sen. Grassley will take.

(Why is it necessary for the Senate staff to spend its time and money on possible tax law violations? Doesn't the IRS investigate these matters properly? Is this a broad attempt to frighten media ministries into submitting to "guidelines" for behavior on/off their broadcasts? When did government receive a "conscience" and from whom did it receive it? Does this mean that the ministries in question must provide their own rope if there is a lynching?)

Q4. Will the committee have hearings on this topic?

A4. As ranking member, Sen. Grassley performs oversight through many means. Correspondence is the most common and often the most effective way of conducting oversight. Interviews of interested parties and witnesses have been helpful as well. Whether there is merit to having a hearing will depend on how the investigation unfolds and, of course, the consideration of the committee chairman.

Q5. Will Sen. Grassley or others propose legislation dealing with ministries?

A5. Whether any legislation is necessary will depend on the findings of the investigations and also the ministries' responses. Sen. Grassley has been very effective in encouraging non-profit groups to perform significant reforms on their own initiative after he [has] brought to light issues of concern. Examples are the Nature Conservancy, Red Cross, United Way, and the Smithsonian. All of these organizations conducted extensive reforms after Sen. Grassley's oversight. (Of note, only one of those involved a hearing, and that was on the Nature Conservancy, after reforms already were in place.)

(Note that none of these ministries under review are members of the Evangelical Council for Financial Accountability (ECFA) or other oversight group. Does that mean that one must pay the price to be an ECFA member or member of some other oversight group to avoid such investigations?)

Q6. What is Sen. Grassley's goal – to get ministries to comply with the law as it's currently written, or to show members of Congress that ministries can perform in ways that other non-profits can't and maybe should face more transparency, at least?

A6. Both. Sen. Grassley hopes all ministries comply with the current tax law. However, it may be that the law, enforcement of the law, and oversight have not kept up with a rapidly changing field. Based on initial review, the way ministries operate has changed significantly over the last 20 years to 25 years, while the tax laws governing them for the most part have not. Media-oriented ministry, formerly referred to as televangelism, is now a billion-dollar industry that receives little or no oversight by the IRS, the organization responsible for enforcing the tax laws. The IRS's tax-exempt and government entities division has been unable to keep up with the exponential growth of all tax-exempt organizations, including churches and ministries. Since ministries, several of which operate under the auspices of a church, are not required to file Form 990 like other non-profit organizations, taxpayers have no idea how their tax-exempt dollars are being spent. In addition, some ministries refuse to provide donors and other interested parties a detailed accounting of how they spend donations, thereby making it nearly impossible to determine if they are adhering to the tax laws.

Across the broad spectrum of media-oriented ministries, it appears that at least several ministers are operating more like corporate CEOs, living in million-dollar mansions and driving $100,000 cars with very little accountability to donors or to the government. Not only is there a transparency issue, but also there are concerns that several ministries appear to have little or no real board governance. In those cases, the board of directors appears to be comprised of family members and close friends who in some cases receive some type of benefit by being on the board. In addition, some ministries also operate publishing companies, recording studios and a host of for-profit companies for which there is little or no oversight. Sen. Grassley hopes to bring these issues to light not only to Congress, but also to taxpayers as well. That's been his goal for all of his scrutiny of non-profit practices in various fields over the past several years.

(Apparently all the government wants to do is control or confiscate the money. Remember to always follow the money. Notice that A6 tells us that the "way ministries operate has changed . . . while the tax laws . . . have not." Does that mean that new tax laws should be written to bring more money into the government now that "televangelism" has big bucks?

Do taxpayers need to know how money is spent in a church? Is it any of their concern? Shouldn't those who give have a right to know where their money is going, so they can give less or give more to the effort? Why should you care how much the local church's minister receives as compensation when you have never given a dime to that church? What business is it of any private citizen, or any government bureaucrat, to know the inner financial workings of a local church in which they have no personal investment?)

Q7. Does Sen. Grassley anticipate sending more letters – is this a rolling project?

A7. Although Sen. Grassley currently has no plans to send any additional letters, the door is open for additional inquiries as needed. As previously stated, he and his staff have received reports of abuses and possible tax violations by numerous ministries. Typically, once an investigation gets under way, various interested parties send additional material to the committee.

(The door is wide open to investigate, humiliate, and confiscate.)

Q8. Do we know of instances of the federal tax code being violated, skirted, or abused, either covered in the six letters or beyond?

A8. As previously stated, it has been reported to Sen. Grassley that there has been substantial abuse of the tax law by several ministries. There is a broad range of alleged abuses, including excessive executive compensation; excessive parsonage allowances; parsonage allowances for family members; the personal use of assets belonging to the tax-exempt organization; the transfer of assets; and unreported income. It appears that several ministers are treating these ministries as if they are their private companies. However, there are specific tax laws that govern tax-exempt organizations, and Sen. Grassley wants to ensure that ministries are adhering to the laws applicable to them. The federal tax code speaks specifically to the prohibition of private inurement and private benefit. This means that the assets and income of a tax-exempt organization are to be dedicated solely for the benefit of a broad charitable class of beneficiaries – that is, the public. In other words, there is to be no element of private gain. The thought is clear in a declaration of the IRS Office of the Chief Counsel: "The inurement prohibition serves to prevent anyone in position to do so from siphoning off any of a charity's income or assets for personal use." As mentioned earlier, in addition to clear instances of illegality, Sen. Grassley intends to explore instances in which activities may be allowable under the law but go against commonly used principles of appropriate conduct for tax-exempt groups in exchange for the billions of dollars of tax breaks they receive.

(Senator Grassley plans to investigate legal activities and make them appear illegal? Whose "commonly used principles" will be used? From which denomination, family, party, or part of society will the principles be taken?)

Response from elements of the Christian establishment was varied, but nearly all sounded the same alarm. The investigation of any church or related ministry opens the possibility for abuse of that ministry and any other Christian church or ministry.

The attorney for New Birth Missionary Baptist Church, James M. Hunter, wrote in the *Atlanta Journal Constitution* on January 6, 2008, that while the church had responded to Senator Grassley's request, they were concerned about their privacy rights. Hunter stated,

" . . . the church insists upon the preservation of the religious freedoms guaranteed by the First and Fourteenth Amendments to the Constitution. We respect Grassley's stated intentions, but we also are concerned about his public media campaign and disregard of the privacy rights afforded New Birth under law. . . . Grassley's public inquiry and accompanying media campaign trample upon protections afforded by both the First Amendment and the Church Audit Procedures Act. Our democracy is founded upon a system of checks and balances, and we should all be concerned when a member of Congress seeks to assume powers that have been assigned to another branch of government. . . . But Grassley's inquiry isn't just an issue for media-based ministries. It's a threat to all religious organizations."

Matthew 6:25-34:

25 "Therefore I say unto you, Take no thought for your life, what ye shall eat, or what ye shall drink; nor yet for your body, what ye shall put on. Is not the life more than meat, and the body than raiment?

26 Behold the fowls of the air: for they sow not, neither do they reap, nor gather into barns; yet your heavenly Father feedeth them. Are ye not much better than they?

27 Which of you by taking thought can add one cubit unto his stature?

2829 And why take ye thought for raiment? Consider the lilies of the field, how they grow; they toil not, neither do they spin: 29 And yet I say unto you, That even Solomon in all his glory was not arrayed like one of these.

30 Wherefore, if God so clothe the grass of the field, which to day is, and to morrow is cast into the oven, shall he not much more clothe you, O ye of little faith?

31-32 Therefore take no thought, saying, What shall we eat? or, What shall we drink? or, Wherewithal shall we be clothed? 32 (For after all these things do the Gentiles seek:) for your heavenly Father knoweth that ye have need of all these things.

33 But seek ye first the kingdom of God, and his righteousness; and all these things shall be added unto you.

34 Take therefore no thought for the morrow: for the morrow shall take thought for the things of itself. Sufficient unto the day is the evil thereof."

Some Church Leaders Fail to See the Dangers of Government Oversight of the Church

While attempting to call for his readers not to demonize Senator Grassley for his investigation (as detailed in the prior chapter), the editor of *Charisma* Magazine, J. Lee Grady, wrote in the November 11, 2007, edition, *"Why are we so paranoid?"*

He wrote that Grassley was an outspoken evangelical Christian and doesn't want the government to intrude into religion. Grady stated, "Grassley has a reputation for integrity. He recently conducted an investigation of several secular nonprofit organizations including the Smithsonian Institution and the American Red Cross. Those entities were not shut down because of his inquiry, but they did make internal changes in order to correct financial abuses and to comply with IRS rules. All Grassley wants is assurance that the six ministries are following the law. Is that evil?"

The *Tampa Tribune* in its November 6, 2007, edition described Grady as "calling for financial reform in Christian evangelical circles."

"This is an awkward time for the church," Grady said. "I believe God is putting his finger on some problems and demanding that we set our house in order. If we don't correct these problems ourselves, then the government may have to step in and do it. And that will be unfortunate."

In a November 12, 2007, open letter regarding J. Lee Grady's response to the Grassley Investigation, Paul Crouch, Jr., Chief of Staff of the Trinity Broadcasting Network, wrote:

"His recent editorial about U.S. Senator Chuck Grassley's call for an investigation of the finances of several prominent television ministries is something that could not only harm the church as we know it today, but the body of Christ as a whole.

"On the surface, the Senate Finance Committee's investigation (and let's call it by its real intent: an inquisition) headed up by Senator Grassley might sound logical, and to some Christians maybe even a good idea. But the long-term effects of this investigation could be devastating. Put aside your personal opinions about any of the six ministries being targeted, and forget how you feel about Christian television as a whole. The much bigger questions we should all be asking are: Do we want the government deciding anything when it comes to the faith we all hold dear? Should government be allowed to dictate what kind of car a minister can drive, or how large a house is permissible and even how much a minister may receive as a salary? Do we want to establish another Church of England, or was that why our forefathers came to this nation in the first place? Separation of church and state is a foundational principle guaranteed in our Constitution, and Mr. Grady's editorial seems to be ignorant of that fact!

" . . . When it comes to 'accountability,' I also take issue with Mr. Grady. Whether you agree with the philosophy or theology of anyone in the pulpit or on Christian TV is not the point. It doesn't matter if they preach the prosperity Gospel and live in mansions, or the poverty Gospel and are all beggars. We must keep the government OUT of the church, or everything our founding fathers fought for is lost! The concept that God would use a senator to 'bring on a reformation,' as Mr. Grady proclaims, is scary and ignorant of the facts. We are dealing with spiritual warfare here, and we must fight back. None of these ministries are required by law to do anything in response to Senator Grassley's investigation, and I hope they don't. All of us in the ministry answer to the IRS, franchise tax boards, county taxing authorities, etc., and that is sufficient oversight. I don't care if Benny Hinn flies in a private plane, or if Creflo Dollar drives a Bentley. That's between them and God. We as Christians are required to give—it's an intrinsic part of our faith. God gave his best to redeem our souls, his only Son, and we are to do the same . . ."

Galatians 6:1-10
1 Brethren, if a man be overtaken in a fault, ye which are spiritual, restore such an one in the spirit of meekness; considering thyself, lest thou also be tempted. 2 Bear ye one another's burdens, and so fulfil the law of Christ. 3 For if a man think himself to be something, when he is nothing, he deceiveth himself. 4 But let every man prove his own work, and then shall he have rejoicing in himself alone, and not in another. 5 For every man shall bear his own burden. 6 Let him that is taught in the word communicate unto him that teacheth in all good things. 7 Be not deceived; God is not mocked: for whatsoever a man soweth, that shall he also reap. 8 For he that soweth to his flesh shall of the flesh reap corruption; but he that soweth to the Spirit shall of the Spirit reap life everlasting. 9 And let us not be weary in well doing: for in due season we shall reap, if we faint not. 10 As we have therefore opportunity, let us do good unto all men, especially unto them who are of the household of faith.

The *Tampa Tribune* (November 6, 2007) quoted the President of the Evangelical Council for Financial Accountability, Kenneth Behr, as saying that the inquiry is "a very big deal. . . . I think he's picking a fight. . . . He is not just asking them to come in and talk, he is asking them for everything." And if they don't tell all, he predicted, Grassley could ask the IRS to step in. "An IRS audit is not pleasant," said the former Ford Motor Co. executive. "I wouldn't wish it on my enemy."

The *Christian Science Monitor* in its December 6, 2007, edition quoted the Senior Vice-President and General Counsel of the National Religious Broadcasters (NRB), Craig Parshall as saying, "There is financial information in an employment contract but also a lot of information that's none of the government's business. . . . There are thousands of Christian ministries engaged in electronic communications who are doing the right things—agonizing about how they are going to use donor dollars. Then you have, perhaps, a handful that have abused the tax laws. That's how bad laws get made."

The article also quoted Brent Walker, Executive Director of the Baptist Joint Committee in Washington, which advocates religious liberty: "Anytime a Congressional committee gets involved in this kind of issue, a red flag goes up. A lot of us are not enamored with the prosperity gospel, but this is not a decision for government to make. Government is supposed to enforce the law evenhandedly, not get involved in picking and choosing the best expression of religion."

In an email from Craig Parshall to this author on January 16, 2008, Parshall wrote that the NRB "has concerns about Senator Grassley's investigation because:

(1) It supersedes the IRS audit and investigation function which, by the way, must be conducted confidentially (as contrasted with the Senator's highly public investigation); further, the IRS is required to comport with guidelines set by Congress itself that require that agency, among other things, to hold pre-audit conferences with the religious organization under audit;

(2) The information broadly requested by Senator Grassley exceeded the financial issues that led to the investigation, and involved subject areas protected by the religion clauses of the First Amendment;

(3) This investigation may be the first step in a process that will lead to Congressional law-making which could impose internal governance rules on non-profit religious groups, something which would likely run afoul of the First Amendment's prohibition against excessive entanglement between State and Church."

2 Corinthians 9:1-15

1 For as touching the ministering to the saints, it is superfluous for me to write to you: 2 For I know the forwardness of your mind, for which I boast of you to them of Macedonia, that Achaia was ready a year ago; and your zeal hath provoked very many. 3 Yet have I sent the brethren, lest our boasting of you should be in vain in this behalf; that, as I said, ye may be ready: 4 Lest haply if they of Macedonia come with me, and find you unprepared, we (that we say not, ye) should be ashamed in this same confident boasting. 5 Therefore I thought it necessary to exhort the brethren, that they would go before unto you, and make up beforehand your bounty, F21 whereof ye had notice before, that the same might be ready, as a matter of bounty, and not as of covetousness.

6 But this I say, He which soweth sparingly shall reap also sparingly; and he which soweth bountifully shall reap also bountifully. 7 Every man according as he purposeth in his heart, so let him give; not grudgingly, or of necessity: for God loveth a cheerful giver. 8 And God is able to make all grace abound toward you; that ye, always having all sufficiency in all things, may abound to every good work: 9 (As it is written, He hath dispersed abroad; he hath given to the poor: his righteousness remaineth for ever. 10 Now he that ministereth seed to the sower both minister bread for your food, and multiply your seed sown, and increase the fruits of your righteousness;) 11 Being enriched in every thing to all bountifulness, F22 which causeth through us thanksgiving to God. 12 For the administration of this service not only supplieth the want of the saints, but is abundant also by many thanksgivings unto God; 13 Whiles by the experiment of this ministration they glorify God for your professed subjection unto the gospel of Christ, and for your liberal distribution unto them, and unto all men; 14 And by their prayer for you, which long after you for the exceeding grace of God in you. 15 Thanks be unto God for his unspeakable gift.

Dr. Phil Cooke, a filmmaker and media activist, posted the following on his website, www.philcooke.com, concerning the threat from the Grassley investigation:

"One of the things that's most disconcerting to me during the Senator Charles Grassley affair is just how little unity there is in the church today. It's no wonder we're not making more of a cultural impact. . . . when a politician targets a large group of people from any faith, it should be a cause for alarm. I'm surprised about two things:

"1. Without being melodramatic, it's apparent that Christians are the only group in America that can be criticized without fear. . . . if Grassley had rounded up six of the top gay and lesbian, African American, Hispanic, Muslim, or other groups, the outcry in the media would be deafening. There's no question it's a sad state for Christianity in America.

"2. I'm also surprised that Christians themselves have not risen up in protest. We raise millions of dollars to protest movies, TV programs, abortion, and plenty of other things, but when a politician targets a group of ministries that represent millions of believers in this country, who's next? Sure—you may not like Creflo Dollar, Benny Hinn, or Eddie Long, but who's next? If we let this happen, when will the government target the Baptists for their position on gender issues, or the Amish for being pacifist during a time of war, or other groups for any number of issues?

"I'm reminded of the classic quote from Martin Niemoeller:

'First they came for the Communists but I was not a Communist so I did not speak out. Then they came for the Socialists and the Trade Unionists but I was not one of them, so I did not speak out. Then they came for the Jews but I was not Jewish so I did not speak out. And when they came for me, there was no one left to speak out for me.'

"This is a wake-up call for unity in the Body of Christ—for a greater sense of community among the body of believers. . . ."

It is not the place, prerogative, or privilege of government to meddle into the affairs of the Church. The First Amendment gives the guarantee of our free expression of religion. If reform is needed, and it appears to most observers that it is, then it should begin and end with the Church.

Senator Grassley's investigation is an indication of things ominous and yet future. If the government crosses the line of the First Amendment protection and invades the Church, what is to keep them from taking away all freedom of religion? What will keep the government from taking away all freedom of speech and right of assembly? What will be the next freedom to fall?

That is why it is important to know the attacks of the bureaucrats and the government elite upon our basic freedoms. We must be informed. Then we must resist their attempts to steal our freedoms. How can we be informed if our lines of communication are cut? If the "Fairness Doctrine" with all its dangers becomes re-established, *how will we know what is really happening in our world?*

CHAPTER

13

The Challenge Before Us

As I stated at the beginning of this book, the "Fairness Doctrine" was never intended to be fair or lead to fairness in broadcasting. It was conceived as a method of taming the conversation of the broadcaster and placing a chill upon the broadcaster to effect a silencing of the truth. President Truman and his minions wanted to ensure that no Washington government would ever be put out of power by the public invested with the truth. They wanted to keep the public from knowing about their escapades, mistakes, communist threats, and internal government turmoil. They especially wanted to put a lid on any Christian evangelistic fundamentalist fervor that might spill over into the political arena. It was the fear in the hearts of the politicians that forged the "Fairness Doctrine." Fear of the people is a potent force when you have things to hide and lies to spread. Perhaps it was more than a basic fear of the voting public. Perhaps it was simply fear of the Truth.

The possible re-imposition of the "Fairness Doctrine" will bring fear, not to the politicians and elitists, but to the broadcasters and ultimately to the average citizen. Lest you think it is simply this author's opinion, read what others are saying about the matter.

Cliff Kincaid, editor of Accuracy in Media's *AIM Report*, has written in the August 2007 issue of *Liberty Journal* about a more sinister design occurring in the quest to silence conservative talk radio.

In the article titled, "The Fairness Doctrine is Not Dead," Mr. Kincaid reported that Democrats are further "paving the way for reinstatement of the Fairness Doctrine" by requesting a federal study of how "broadcast facilities licensed on behalf of the public by the Federal Communications Commission" have been used to "convey messages of bigotry or hatred, creating a climate of fear and inciting individuals to commit hate crimes."

In other words, if Democrats can't cut into the ratings of conservative radio leaders, they want to be able to insinuate that their words are harmful to the national welfare.

Mr. Kincaid reported that Reps. John D. Dingell, chairman of the House Energy and Commerce Committee, and Edward J. Markey, chairman of the House Subcommittee on Telecommunications and the Internet, made the request in a letter to John M.R. Kneuer, Assistant Secretary for Communications and Information at the National Telecommunications and Information Administration.

"The obvious purpose of such a study," he wrote, "is to produce 'evidence' that could lead to laws, policies or regulations, such as the Fairness Doctrine, to silence broadcasters perceived or alleged to be behind 'hate crimes.' Religious broadcasters who oppose liberal and promiscuous lifestyles would be a natural target. It is apparent that the Left is serious about eradicating the enormous influence of conservative talk radio."

The following were quoted in the *Liberty Journal:*

Representative Mike Pence (R-IN) and author of the Broadcaster Freedom Act that prohibits the FCC from reinstating the "Fairness Doctrine" has said, "Unless Congress addresses this threat to free speech, any future administration could impose this unfair doctrine upon America with the stroke of a pen."

Representative Connie Mack (R-FL) has stated, "The free flow of information is essential to a flourishing democracy, and a free and independent press serves as a vital check on the government. The Fairness Doctrine amounts to nothing short of government censorship and control of the airwaves, and walks a dangerous line toward government rationing of free speech."

Senator John Kyl (R-AZ) remarked, "Some Democrats may not like talk radio, but that does not give them the right to use the heavy hand of government to regulate it. Americans have always fiercely believed in the fundamental importance of a free and independent press. As Thomas Jefferson once said, 'Our liberty depends on the freedom of the press, and that cannot be limited without being lost.'"

Pastor Jonathan Falwell of the Thomas Road Baptist Church, Lynchburg, Virginia, speaks of personal experience when he says, "In Canada, where radical doctrines have already taken hold, our ministry's television broadcast has for years faced censorship of any reference that was deemed to be politically incorrect. Liberal forces in Washington would like nothing better than to similarly restrict or silence the ministries and pulpits of pro-family and pro-life voices like Dr. James Dobson, Dr. John Hagee, Dr. Franklin Graham or any Bible-preaching pastor."

Representative David Davis (R-TN) in conversation with the author stated, "The prospect of the 'Fairness Doctrine' being resurrected is one that is abhorrent to those that love truth and freedom. Should the Democrats get their way and pass hate crimes legislation or reinstate the 'Fairness Doctrine,' we will suffer as a nation because the truth will be in short supply on the nation's airwaves. Talk shows, news, and Christian programs will be a thing of the past. We must make sure that never happens."

The "Fairness Doctrine" was ill conceived and it was proper for it to have been abandoned by the FCC and its regulators. It should never again be forced upon the broadcasters and the American public.

Make no mistake. Even though it was a burden to the broadcaster and prohibited free expression on the airwaves, the Democrats and Washington elitists will not rest until, once again, they restrict your freedoms with the "Fairness Doctrine" or its offspring.

We must not rest. We must work to ensure that the "Fairness Doctrine" and other such encroachments upon the First Amendment are destroyed.

CHAPTER

14

What Can We Do?

First of all, contact your member of Congress and the Office of the President. Tell them *you do not want the* "Fairness Doctrine."

An e-mail is received much quicker than using the postal service. With the various terrorism scares, regular mail must be screened and it could take several weeks to reach the intended recipient.

If you are going to use the postal service and you are writing your Congressman or Senator you should use the district office address that is nearest you. This will allow for a quicker receipt of your letter.

Your letter or e-mail should be brief and cordial. Usually there is no advantage to write more than one page in a 12-point type. There is no need for a full dissertation on the subject. If you think more information is needed, send a copy of this book in a separate package following your letter. If you send the book, make sure you inform them in the letter that the book will be sent.

When you write, be sure to use your own words. Having read this book, you should have enough information to relate the problems with the "Fairness Doctrine" and why you want your President, Representative, and/or Senators to be against it as well.

Be respectful and polite. Proverbs 25:11 & 12 remind us: *"A word fitly spoken is like apples of gold in pictures of silver. As an earring of gold, and an ornament of fine gold, so is a wise reprover upon an obedient ear."*

You may send your comments to the President by mail at:
The White House
1600 Pennsylvania Avenue NW
Washington, DC 20500
Or by email at comments@whitehouse.gov

You may email your Member of the
House of Representatives by visiting:
http://www.house.gov/writerep
Or, to find your Representative's office and address:
http://www.house.gov/house/Memberwww_by_State.shtml

You may email your Member of the Senate by going to:
http://www.senate.gov/general/contact_information/senators_cfm.cfm

Research this and other issues facing these United States.

- Pray for wisdom.

- Read.

- Be active in your community.

- Be informed about life in general and your life, specifically.

- Attend public forums, lectures, town hall meetings, city council sessions, political party functions, seminars, and conferences.

- In your research, do not accept everything you hear as being the truth.

Verify your sources and know the bias of the verified sources. You must be vigilant at all times. Do not use the Internet or talk radio as your only source of information. Again, verify your sources and know which sources you can trust.

Check everything you read, study, hear, and learn by the truth found in

God's Word. When in doubt, read the book of Proverbs. This is God's instruction on how to live life on a daily basis.

Read your Bible daily and you will be less likely to be fooled into believing the world's lies. Remember John 8:32: *"And ye shall know the truth, and the truth shall make you free."*

Vote intelligently and righteously.
Before you vote, be sure to have done your homework on candidates and issues.

Luke 14: 28, 31 asks these questions: *"For which of you, intending to build a tower, sitteth not down first, and counteth the cost, whether he have sufficient to finish it? 31 Or what king, going to make war against another king, sitteth not down first, and consulteth whether he be able with ten thousand to meet him that cometh against him with twenty thousand?"*

Will you build a structure without making plans and figuring the cost? Will you expend your strength and give your life without knowing what you face in the struggle?

Our votes should not be cast without the same diligence.

We also should know what belongs to the government (the vote) and what belongs to God (ourselves and everything we have). Mark 12:17 – *"And Jesus answering said unto them, Render to Caesar the things that are Caesar's, and to God the things that are God's. And they marvelled at him."*

Speak the truth at all times, in love, but in a fashion to be heard and understood.
Be careful to present your case in as gentle and as firm a fashion as is possible. If you are active in the community, you will have the opportunity to speak concerning important issues.

We gain insight as to this process in the writing of the Apostle Paul. He wrote in Romans 12: 17-19: *"Recompense to no man evil for evil. Provide things honest in the sight of all men. If it be possible, as much as lieth in you, live peaceably with all men. Dearly beloved, avenge not yourselves, but rather give place unto wrath: for it is written, Vengeance is mine; I will repay, saith the Lord."*

When Paul was writing to Pastor Titus he told him what to teach the people so they could live good lives; and then he added in Titus 2:15: *"These things speak, and exhort, and rebuke with all authority. Let no man despise thee."*

Support those broadcast stations and programs that tell the truth. Pray for them. Write to them and encourage them. If they are non-profit ministries, support them with your giving.
Galatians 6:6 instructs: *"Let him that is taught in the word communicate unto him that teacheth in all good things."*

If you are taught, then it is your obligation to let the teacher know that you have received the message. The word "communicate" in this verse means more than just "send a letter" or "make a phone call." It also means to contribute to the welfare of the one that teaches.

If you have learned from this book, recommend it to others. You may even buy a copy or two for your friends.

If a commercial broadcast station has informational programs that keep you informed, be sure to buy from their advertisers and let the advertisers know why you are buying from them.

If a listener-supported broadcast facility has taught you and helped you in your daily life, give a gift of money or volunteer your time or talent to their outreach.

Pray for those who teach you.

A letter is a great way to let them know that you have been taught.

Tell others to do the same.

Use your freedom of speech to instruct others and help them become involved as guardians of the freedoms that God has given to each of us.

"No man is entitled to the blessings of freedom unless he be vigilant in its preservation."--General Douglas MacArthur

"History does not long entrust the care of freedom to the weak or the timid." --President Dwight Eisenhower

"If you will not fight for the right when you can easily win without bloodshed; if you will not fight when your victory will be sure and not too costly, you may come to the moment when you will have to fight with all the odds against you and only a small chance of survival. There may even be a worse case: you may have to fight when there is no hope of victory, because it is better to perish than to live as slaves."--Sir Winston Churchill

"The jaws of power are always open to devour, and her arm is always stretched out, if possible, to destroy the freedom of thinking, speaking, and writing." --John Adams

"Our natural, inalienable rights are now considered to be a dispensation from government; and freedom has never been so fragile, so close to slipping from our grasp as it is at this moment."--Ronald Reagan

The "Fairness Doctrine": A History of Abuse

The following is a transcript of three interviews conducted in 1994 by the Author with Rev. Jim Nicholls. The interviews provide interesting insight from one who had been the victim of the Fairness Doctrine.

Kenneth C. Hill – Rev. Jim Nicholls is vice-president of WGCB in Red Lion, Pennsylvania. He is heard regularly on the "Voice of Freedom" broadcast, both on radio and television. He also has another television program called "Capital Insight" that he hosts. We will be discussing the so-called Fairness Doctrine.

Jim, when does your contact with the so-called Fairness Doctrine begin?

Jim Nicholls – It goes back into the 1960s.

Hill – Tell me a little bit about the so-called Fairness Doctrine – how was it used against Christians?

Nicholls – When you check through the stations that have been involved with challenges on the Fairness Doctrine, it is basically the God-and-country type stations. Many will recall Dr. Carl McIntyre and the station that was actually owned by Faith Theological Seminary, WXUR. This station was challenged, as my station KAYE was, out in the state of Washington. I stood very strongly for God and country.

Both WXUR and my station were commercial stations that were designed to program for the community, but we did carry some Christian programming on them. I mean, we weren't one hundred percent Christian. My own station, all night long, played Christian music. We had a few vocals; but to me, Christian music is the finest music in the world. So, during the nighttime, that seemed to be a good way of serving the community. But during the daytime, I programmed to try and meet the community needs.

If you meet those needs successfully, and when I say meet them, I mean if you challenge the liberal powers that be—the liberal, socialist point-of-view—then you are in trouble. I was earmarked by thirteen preachers connected with the National Council of Churches who filed against me at license renewal time. The *New York Times* wrote the story that I had too much influence in my community and had to be silenced. Dr. Everett Parker, who was then the executive director of the Broadcast Commission of the United Church of Christ, operated out of New York City. His office filed news releases to The *New York Times* and I guess hundreds of other publications across the country.

Wow! I got a rude awakening. I found out what the Fairness Doctrine was through personal experience. The Fairness Doctrine itself doesn't seem to have a thing wrong with it because it sounds good. It's like apple pie with cheese on it. You know, "apple pie without cheese is like a kiss without a squeeze. Who is against fairness? No one. Nobody.

But when you find out what the Fairness Doctrine is and how it is being interpreted, then, wow! Anybody could be in trouble, depending on who is in power at the present time. There is such latitude of interpretation that the Fairness Doctrine can mean whatever anybody wants it to mean in any given period of time in history. Kenneth, when you stop and think—in order to defend yourself against false charges, you can spend as much as ten times what the station is often worth! You are in a position where there is absolutely no Constitutional protection for you.

I am not sure if you are aware of this, Kenneth, but at the present time, the broadcaster does not have First Amendment rights. This is kind of ironic. A television station can carry programming. Cable systems can pick that programming up and play the exact same things that television stations carry. The cable system is protected by First Amendment rights, but the television station that originated the programming does not have First Amendment rights. That shocks a lot of people. But those are the facts of court records, and it shouldn't be; but that is the way it is. When it comes to even this present time, the broadcaster still does not have First Amendment rights. He does not have, technically speaking, freedom of the press.

When the Broadcast Communications Act of 1934 came into being, Senator Dill from Washington was chairman of the Senate committee that had oversight of writing the bill. He called in one of his legal aides to write the bill. The man that he called in as a legal aide had actually worked with the Utilities Commission. When they tried to write up the Broadcast Communications Act, the only phrase that he could come up with that seemed to sound feasible was a phrase that he borrowed from the Utilities Act, and he wrote it into the Broadcast Act. That phrase was that broadcasters exist to "serve the public interest, convenience, and necessity" of a community. This information surfaced when Newton Minnow was chairman of the FCC. He was very disturbed at the wording of the Broadcast Communications Act, so he called on Senator Dill to find out just how the act came into being and why it was worded the way it was worded.

It came as quite a shock to find that it was actually worded in the phraseology that utilities are worded, and yet broadcast facilities are not utilities. Minnow repeated that two or three times to emphasize it—that the broadcast facility is not a public utility and has no similarity with the utilities like power and light, etc. "Senator Dill," Mr. Minnow continued, "why did you use that phraseology to serve the public interest, convenience, and necessity of the community?"

"Well, because it sounded good. And no one objected to it. And so it was written into law," was the reply of Senator Dill.

"Well, why wasn't there some protection of the Constitution, like freedom of the press, etc.?" asked Minnow.

"Well, uh, no one ever questioned that," replied Dill.

No one ever raised that point. Freedom of the press for broadcasters has never been put into the law. That is the way it stands right now. The Fairness Doctrine took a period of time evolving.

Hill -- The abuse of power by the improper use of the Fairness Doctrine must be devastating.

Nicholls – Kenneth, I actually "died" in the process. A gentleman in Hawaii had similar charges filed against him as I had, and as Dr. McIntyre's station WXUR had. Though he was a millionaire and owned a big department store in Hawaii, he didn't even bother fighting it. He just took his license off the wall and mailed it back to the Commission and just gave up. He said it wasn't worth fighting for. It was such a vicious battle, and he felt money could be spent to better use.

We basically were the three stations that were involved in the Fairness Doctrine. Dr. McIntyre had his WXUR license revoked. I didn't have mine revoked. I "died" in the process.

So, I made history, because I am the only man in history that went through two full-fledged hearings, both of which were aborted. I was slated for a third hearing. The last two hearings were supposed to be under orders of the FCC, with the Administrative Law judge ordered to allow us to present our rebuttal. I have never to this day ever been allowed to present my rebuttal.

Hill – It sounds like a lapse in the justice process. Due process was not followed by the FCC.

Nicholls – Those who brought the challenge against us had none of the charges verified, nor even proven to be reasonable, before we were thrown into a hearing. That is a violation of Constitutional rights. There should be reasonable cause supported by oath or affirmation before a hearing is ordered. And yet that was never done. Just simply because you had some powerful groups like Dr. Everett Parker and the Anti-Defamation League who filed charges, a hearing was ordered. Although the Anti-Defamation League [on] the twelfth day of the hearing pulled out, they went after their own people in the Pacific Northwest. The New York office was very furious with them for supplying them with information that was not supported by factual evidence. It was a cinch [that] I was not anti-Semitic.

Hill – Was it a sense of "Let's get these do-gooding Bible thumpers, and get them off the air, because they are going to ruin our society"?

Nicholls – We need to go back to the fact of the historical setting at that time. The Vietnam War was there. I think it was the *TV Guide* of February 1972, if my memory holds good, where Mr. Howard K. Smith, the famed commentator at that time, stated that we broadcasters, referring basically to the news media, did not tell the American public the whole truth. All we did was tell the American public one side. We kept harping away and harping away and we split America right down the middle. Now the Fairness Doctrine was in vogue, but it was never used against the liberal Left. It was only used against those who were basically for God-and-country.

Hill – Why do you think that happened? Was there a conspiracy indeed from all these organizations getting together, or just misinformation? What was going on?

Nicholls – I was considered to be the number-one authority on the Fairness Doctrine in this country. You may have heard of Ray Bream and his talk show out in Los Angeles. That's the ABC flagship station out of Los Angeles. I don't know about his program now, but back in that period of time it was the number-one moneymaking talk show in America. He brought me out to Los Angeles because he was having so much trouble from college professors in the Los Angeles area where there are so many colleges—and most of the colleges were of a liberal, socialist bent or slant. They were calling in on his program and giving them trouble, so Ray brought me out there because he recognized me as the number-one authority on the Fairness Doctrine. It was quite a show. I had the honor of being on his show longer than he had ever had any man on at one given time. Next time I was back, I was on for the full length of his show, from beginning to end. At that time, he had never had anyone on for that period of time. I say that just to give some credibility to what I am saying.

Your question had to do with "Why?" Was there a conspiracy? First of all, I would say, maybe only God knows the truth. We can put two and two together and think it comes up with four. Whether that [conspiracy theory] is true or not, I don't know. But there was a working together of certain people that supported a liberal-socialist cause. In my particular case, you had the Ford Foundation giving to the Broadcast Commission of the United Church of Christ several hundred thousand dollars that was used to destroy me. I am certain if Henry Ford that started the whole Ford empire had been alive, he would be horrified to think that his money and his foundation were being used to destroy the very thing that he had believed in.

The AFL-CIO was also used. Their first check to Dr. Parker's group was, I think, for $85,000. I was considered the voice of the laboring man out in the Puget Sound area. Overnight, I put into our state capital in the state of Washington, which is Olympia, the largest crowd that had ever been brought into Olympia. The laboring people considered me their voice. They were horrified when they found out that their own union had taken $85,000 of their money to try and destroy the only voice they had at that time in the Pacific Northwest.

There you have powerful groups. But those groups apparently were working in conjunction with [those of] the social, liberal bent—certainly not with the God-and-country people. Now, when I say God-and-country, maybe I should clarify that. This country basically was started as a declared Christian country, with a declared Christian purpose. It is up to you and me to keep it Christian, because if we don't, pray tell me who will? We are either one nation under God, or we are one nation under. And we better not kid ourselves; that's the way it is. That last statement I gave you, "We're either one national under God or we're one nation under," came from no less a personage than President Ronald Reagan himself.

Hill – When this was going on and all of these powerful groups were putting in money that had been taken from their constituents to silence the station that you were with, what was the battle? How was the battle drawn? How did you go about defending yourself?

Nicholls – That's the problem. We were never allowed to defend ourselves. We had an Administrative Law judge that was very prejudiced, and I was never allowed to defend myself. The plaintiffs could say anything they liked without proof. The former general counsel of the FCC, who had written many of the rules, regulations, and laws of the FCC, Ben Catoni, was my attorney. He knew the FCC rules and laws forward and backward. Anytime he tried to demand proof, the attorney called him out of order. It's a hearing the like of which you'll never find recorded in hearing history.

Hill – Is this the kind of thing that will happen again if the Fairness Doctrine is put back into effect?

Nicholls – I am sure it will be, because there are no qualifications. There are no clarifications. There are no interpretations.

There is one thing more I should tell you about the history of the Fairness Doctrine. Let me tell you, to my knowledge, the first Fairness Doctrine ruling that we ever had, had to do with a good ol' Baptist Texan by the name of Sam Morris. You may have heard of Sam Morris. He was called the "Voice of Temperance." He was like Billy Sunday. He would fight the devil booze until Hell froze over, and then he would go after him on the ice! He really had quite a radio program back in those days, called the "Voice of Temperance." When I first met Sam, I was at Winona Lake in the Billy Sunday Tabernacle. Sam Morris was preaching that night; it was a Sunday night. He looked up, and he started to look at that congregation, and there were many preachers and Christian workers, because this was a conference on evangelism.

He started over to his left, and as he started over the congregation, he said, "You people. You're nothing but a bunch of cowards. You call yourself Christian and you oughta be ashamed of yourself." He was going across the audience, going from left to right. "Where you should have a backbone, you have a jellybone." And he just went down all the way across the audience, and then back again. Just downranking them. I guess they needed it. Then he said, "It's because of people like you that we here in America are losing our freedom. You want to know why I'm so angry and mad? I'll tell you." He said, "On Tuesday morning, I am to meet with the Senate. I have been kicked off the air. Why have I been kicked off the air? Because I believe that booze is one of the biggest enemies that this country has. Now, the booze crowd is allowed to be on the air and advertise their wares; but I can't go on the air, because I tell the evil of what drink will do to America. Now, I challenged this. So the Senate has arranged for a committee hearing and I am to meet with them Tuesday morning."

This is what Sam did. Sam went into that hearing way back in the mid-1940s. He said, "Gentlemen (talking to the Senate Committee), I am Sam Morris. I am known as the 'Voice of Temperance.' But I am not allowed on the radio because I speak against drinking. I tell people not to drink." And then he pointed over to the men (I'm using Sam's language here now), "These people over here are allowed to go on any station in America and tell people to drink their brand. They tell people that their brand is the best of all of them. They have not even agreed amongst themselves as to what is the best brand to drink, but they are allowed to go on any station and advertise their wares. I am not allowed to go on there and tell them not to drink. They're allowed to tell them to drink. Now, gentlemen, I want you to answer me one question. What is the most controversial? To tell people to drink, or tell them not to drink?"

Now, that is where the Senate came up with their first ruling. They said that any station that accepts liquor advertising must give Sam Morris equal time to present his point of view, not to drink. Now the Senate passed that ruling, but it wasn't lived up to. The liquor crowd was able to advertise. So a few year later, *Newsweek* came up with a great big story where Sam Morris was suing the liquor trade and certain broadcasters for multi-million dollars—which at that time was a tremendous suit—for denying him the right of access to airwaves.

Hill – What happened after that? In the working through of this Fairness

Doctrine, what went on?

Nicholls – The Fairness Doctrine itself is a very simple doctrine. It simply says that when there is a discussion of a controversial issue of public importance and an attack is made on an identifiable person or a group or organization as to its character, honesty, or other personal qualities, then that person must be notified, telling them what was said about them and then give them an opportunity to respond. Now, that sounds good. Great! I don't know of a single broadcaster that would be opposed to that.

Hill – I don't either, Jim, and that's why some people ask me, why are you speaking out against such a "good" thing?

Nicholls – Let me tell you why. This country was started as a Christian country with a declared Christian purpose. You can check through the original charters of the colonies. There you will find that this country was started for the glory of God and "for the propagation of the Gospel of Jesus Christ" and "to bring infidels and savages to civility"—and of course, that is through the preaching of the Gospel. Now these are some of the declared purposes of why this country came into being. The only established religion that this country has ever had is Christianity. It was established long before there was any such thing as a First Amendment. In fact, our whole judicial system is based on God's law, Common Law. That was the system of law that the founding fathers used when they set up our judicial system in this country. Common Law, according to Blackstone, is nothing more than the Christians' Bible.

Where did Common Law come from, except you trace this all the way back to the nomadic tribes of Israel when God gave His law from Mount Sinai? As some of the tribes dispersed, some went north, some went west, and through posterity, everywhere they went they left behind them God's law which is the Common Law for mankind. And finally they landed. When I say "they," I'm talking about posterity [descendants of ancient Israeli tribes] and this is what history books will tell us. They brought to England the Common Law. There the Common Law was made the big thing. When our founding fathers came to this country, they brought with them the Common Law.

At the founding of this country there were only two law systems that were basically known to our founding fathers. One was the law of continental Europe, which was none other than the ancient law of civil Rome. The other law was the English Common Law, and that was what they made the basis of our whole system of jurisprudence. Try to get a Common Law case in the court today. One of the big problems in our courts today is [that] our cases are being decided on civil law, not God's Law or Common Law. Here then is the very foundation of our country: Christianity.

That doesn't mean that we are not going to allow any other religions here, because under the First Amendment, we believe in freedom of religion. Will Ray in the sixties and seventies was chief of the Complaints and Compliance Division of the FCC. I have in writing his own statement: "Anything that is broadcast is subject to the Fairness Doctrine. The preacher's sermon from his church that is broadcast over the air is subject to the Fairness Doctrine."

So, this is what you find yourself with: The scenario [where] if you preach that Jesus is the Christ, the Son of God, the Savior, [then] in essence, you would be forced as a broadcaster to have someone come in and tell you, or tell the audience, that Jesus is *not* the Christ, He is *not* the Son of God, He is *not* the Savior. When you preach that the Bible is God's inspired, inerrant Word . . . you would have to have someone come in there—a Modernist—and tell you, tell the people, your listeners, *"That is only a point-of-view, here's the other side of the coin,"* etc. In other words, you couldn't really preach anything that was absolute or positive. You would have to have a pro and a con. That's the so-called Fairness Doctrine.

Hill – We must realize that we stand for truth, and those that would not stand for truth, stand for error. If it were just talking about daffodils being pretty or not being pretty, that's one thing. But when it is talking about truth, not simply taste or perception, that is something totally different.

Nicholls – That is what people fail to see. Back in that period of time, the broadcasters, they simply followed the line of least resistance. And then when the pressure was put on to be opposed to Vietnam, to make our U.S. Government and forces look bad, the Mai Lai incident was hit on repeatedly, day after day, week after week, month after month. The "atrocities of the Americans"... *boy!* As Howard K. Smith said, because they told only one side, they split America right down the middle, and that wound, to this present day, has never been healed.

Hill – But you know, Jim, if the Fairness Doctrine had been truly enforced and invoked, the other side would have been heard; the atrocities that the Viet Cong and the North Vietnamese were committing would have been seen. The trouble that the people had in the south of Vietnam from the north would have been known.

Nicholls – Kenneth, right there, let me stop you. At the Brookings Institute, which cannot be considered a conservative think-tank by any stretch of the imagination, they did an analysis of the news in America—of ABC, NBC, and CBS—to see just how fair the news was. This had to do with the defense of our nation. There they found that about 98 percent of the news was given to disabuse the American public into thinking that we did not need the armaments and armies that we had [and] we could reduce our military and our defense units. Here we were at war in Vietnam, supposedly, and the whole news media, 98 percent of its time, [worked] to destroy and weaken our military operation.

Now where is the fairness? This was actually taken to court, and figures were shown where 98.2 percent [of media effort] was given to tear down our country, and approximately two percent was given to show that this country needed to be built up and strengthened. The court ruled that none of the networks or stations had to give opposing views. And yet, we had a "Fairness" Doctrine.

Hill – For those who would stand up and be on the side of good and

God, there was a "Fairness" Doctrine, but for those who would be for socialism and for tearing down the country, there was none.

Nicholls – It was only applied to those who had built up influence and seemed to be a threat to the liberal, socialist position. The Fairness Doctrine became a murder weapon that was used to clobber to death points-of-view that seemed to be a threat to the liberal socialists.

Hill – What happened then, after the death of KAYE and the pulling of the license of WXUR, and all the other frightful things that went on during that time—with the abuse of the Fairness Doctrine and the misuse by the various groups against Bible-believing folks—[was] the broadcasters then said, *well, let's just not have any of that. Let's just put on fluffy things, and let's go along with the flow.*

Nicholls – That's right.

Hill – So, this so-called Fairness Doctrine had what has been called a chilling effect on First Amendment-guaranteed freedom of speech, did it not?

Nicholls – I ran out of money; you see, the hearing itself just bled me to death financially. I spent everything I had. I cashed in my bonds and any stocks I had. I cashed in the life insurance policies. To this day, I still have no life insurance policy. I cashed it all in and put it into the battle. We spent basically ten times what it would have cost to buy the station in the first place. We weren't able to even get our defense heard. I just ran out of money and died, so to speak. I packed up and came to Washington, D.C., and started to pound the marble corridors. And there, for about twelve or thirteen years, I got before every Congressional committee I could get before and I taught every Senator's legislative aide and different committees Constitutional law—and told them exactly how things were being used.

I have testified extensively on this. You'll find many, many pages of testimony that I have given. One of the reasons our country is in the mess it is in today is because we who are conservative, and we who are Christians have not been heard. We've been sitting on our apathy--we've been sitting on our duff (pardon my language) but you understand what I am talking about. The Bible says that while good men slept, an enemy came in and sowed seed ... that would destroy the good. And that is what has happened to America.

Paul told the Galatians, "Oh foolish Galatians, who hath bewitched you?" I am sure if Paul were here today and looked at America—and realizing how this country was built on a Biblical foundation—he would look at America, and he would scream out against America, "Oh, foolish Americans, who has bewitched you? Who's hoo-dooed you? Who's pulled the wool over your eyes? You started well, what's wrong with you?"

We have got to get back to our moorings.

I went to Washington, D.C., and I was there less than a month before I met Senator Sam Ervin, who was then in the middle of the Watergate hearings. I worked with his Constitution committee and I was able to have them sponsor a bill, called Senate Bill Two; at least he was *going* to sponsor it, but because the Watergate hearings extended over a period of time, he couldn't sponsor it. So, to my surprise, Senator Proxmire picked up the bill and filed it as Senate Bill Two. This became known as my bill. The biggest shock I think I ever got in my lifetime, was when Father Drinan called me. He was a Congressman, but he was a radical, liberal, Roman Catholic priest. He was a full supporter of the Berrigan brothers—revolutionaries, as they were known at that time. But he got elected to Congress.

This bill, Senate Bill Two, was a very simple bill designed to give the broadcaster First Amendment rights. One day in Washington, D.C., (I had an office in the National Press Building) the phone rang. I answered it. And the voice said, "Is this Rev. Nicholls?"

I said, "Yes."

He said, "This is Father Drinan."

"Who?" I asked.

"You know. You know. Congressman Drinan."

"Oh, yes, Father," I said.

He said, "I called just to let you know what I did with your bill."

"My bill?" I replied. "What do you mean?"

"You know. You know. Senate Bill Two," he said.

"Oh, yes."

He said, "I wanted to let you know that I threw this bill in the hopper on the House side."

"You did what?" I asked.

He said, "I put it in the hopper on the House side. I'm the sponsor of it."

"You are?" I wondered aloud.

"Does that surprise you?" he asked me.

"Yes, it does," I said. "Can you come up and see me?" he then asked me.

"I sure can," I responded.

"When can you come?" he asked.

"You name the time and I will be there," I told him.

We got together and spent some hours together discussing it. The first thing he said to me was, "You seem surprised that I, a liberal out in left field, would support your bill."

I said, "Yes, Congressman, it has really surprised me. I don't think I have ever had a bigger shock in my life than that."

"Well," he said, "let me tell you this. We on the other side of the fence realize now that we need the First Amendment. We need freedom of the press. We have to have Constitutional protection. And that's why I am supporting this bill." He said, "There is one other man in Congress that is way out in right field: Congressman Larry McDonald. Now if you could get him to support this bill, the two of us will become the co-sponsors here. We would have the extreme left and we would have the extreme right. Everybody else, all the Congressmen in between, should serve as sponsors, too."

So I said, "All right, I'll go and see what I can do with Congressman McDonald."

And lo and behold, Congressman Larry McDonald became a co-sponsor. Here you have the sponsorship of both the extreme left and what they called the extreme right. You couldn't get a single broadcaster to take a stand for First Amendment rights for the broadcaster. They were so scared of the FCC. Now isn't that a shame when government can get that stranglehold on the broadcast media?

Hill – Jim, you know the broadcast media has several organizations that the broadcast stations belong to – NAB, NRB and others. You mean, even *those* organizations would not come out in strength on behalf of this?

Nicholls – Let me answer that, and I'll do it very truthfully, even though it may embarrass the NAB. NAB is the National Association of Broadcasters. I sat in the office and talked to their vice-president who was an attorney—and, I must say, a mighty good attorney. He was a Presbyterian. I sat and talked in his office about my problem and needing help. The tears ran down [from] his eyes and he said, "Jim, I would love to help you, but I can't." He said, "If we were to take a stand to support you, what happened to you might happen to any of us."

The National Religious Broadcasters—I went to them. You couldn't get any of them to discuss the issue, so I raised the issue from the floor. And they abruptly adjourned the meeting. I don't know if you were there, but it was abruptly adjourned.

Nicholls – I accused the National Religious Broadcasters of being like a lady's handkerchief—more for show than blow. Once a year they put on a great big meeting, but what does it do the rest of the year? But since then, Dr. Ben Armstrong, former Director of the NRB, and myself have become very close friends.

Presidents of five state broadcasting associations—there, I'm talking about the secular broadcasters—they told me, "Jim, we hope you don't get disgusted in the battle and get tired and fed up and quit. We need you to fight our battle."

Nicholls - I remember, in my own state of Washington, when I talked with the president, those were his very words. He said, "Jim, please don't get disgusted with us or tired in the battle. We need you there to fight our battle." I said, "It gets mighty lonely on the front line. Why don't you join me?"

"No, no. We couldn't do that," he said. "I myself, I am involved personally in five stations. And if we got involved, what has happened to you could happen to every one of us."

Nicholls - I said, "Then, if you can't come and stand with me, why don't you help me pay some bills?"

This president said, "Jim, if it was found out that we gave you so much as one penny, then these forces could turn against any one of us and we could lose everything that we have."

And I said to the fellow, "Well, what do you think I have lost?" That made him sit up and stick his head out. His eyes bugged, and he says, "Yeah, you're right. You are the type of person that can do that. But we can't."

Hill – What happened to Senate Bill Two?

Nicholls – It died. It had hearings and maybe we can go into some of those hearings. Because there I can explain just how the Fairness Doctrine is being used and how few people understand it—even Congress itself

Hill – What happened to the Fairness Doctrine that it is not in force now?

Nicholls – I believe what really happened was the testimony before Congress made Congressmen and Senators realize just how wrong the Fairness Doctrine was. There was nothing fair about it. I remember standing up in the National Religious Broadcasters Convention in Washington, D.C. You may recall the Milam-Landsman petition that was filed with the Commission.

Hill – Right—the one that we still hear so much about. They call it the Madalyn Murray O'Hare Petition. But she had nothing to do with it. We need to tell people right now, there is no such thing as the Madalyn Murray O'Hare Petition before the FCC. Milam-Landsman was a different issue, but it did get confused there, didn't it?

Nicholls – It got confused. These fellows, Milam and Landsman, actually had a station in my backyard in Seattle. They aired a constant diet of obscenities and blasphemies. The Administrative Law judge that held a hearing was the same Administrative Law judge that heard my case. His name was Mr. Nash. He said, about the Milam-Landsman station in Seattle—they had several of them in different parts of the country—"That type of station was needed in America and he hoped there would be more of them."

In other words, it was quite all right for stations to blaspheme, curse, swear, and use obscenities as a constant diet twenty-four hours a day, over the radio. But a God-and-country station? No. There was no room, no place for that kind of station in America. That was an Administrative Law judge that heard cases under the so-called Fairness Doctrine.

Hill – This Administrative Law judge was supposedly fair and unbiased?

Nicholls – Yes. Now that was the way that the Fairness Doctrine was interpreted then. I have had considerable experience testifying in Congress as a result of this. The first time I ever stood in Congress was actually in the Senate before Senator Pastore who had charge as Chairman of the Oversight Committee of the FCC. There my first testimony consisted of about seventy-eight pages plus exhibits. I don't know if you have ever attended any of these hearings, but preceding me were attorneys for CBS, NBC, ABC, Storer, and Westinghouse. Senator Pastore called me up. All these attorneys did was just simply read the statement that they had submitted to the committee twenty-four hours ahead of time in multiples of one hundred copies. The reason they do that is so they have opportunity to have their aides go through [and create] embarrassing questions [to] make you look bad. That's why they are submitted ahead of time.

So, when I took the chair that was vacated, Senator Pastore said, "Reverend, I hope you are not going to read this whole testimony."

I said, "No, sir, I wouldn't dare insult you people, because I am sure you, Mr. Chairman, and members of your committee, are better readers than I could ever hope to be. I want to file it for record."

"So, be it," was what Mr. Pastore said. He speaks that way.
"But, sir, I do have some things I want to say," I said.

Then he said, "Say on."

So, I said, "What makes America different than any other country in the world, is we are under rule of law, not under rule of man."

Then Pastore said, "Reverend, stop! Hold up! Hold up! Stop!"

He is that way. He engaged in theatrics, and I stopped as soon as he said "Reverend."

Then he said, "Sir, I don't know if you realize this or not, but I have been chairman up here for twenty-seven years and you have just made a statement that I never, ever heard anybody make in any of the hearings that I have attended or chaired. That statement that you made, sir, was what makes America different than any other country is that we are under rule of law, not rule of man. Is that correct?"

I said, "Yes, sir."

Then he fired away. "What is rule of law?"

Thank the Lord, I was able to tell him. And they kept me there for almost two hours until lunchtime, and then he wanted me to come back after. And he gave me another hour-and-a-half.

Now all the other men—Westinghouse, NBC—they had from five-to-seven minutes, approximately, that is all they had. Pastore, for the first time in his life, got to see what the Fairness Doctrine was like, and how it was being used. Every single hearing that had anything to do with the FCC, I was there.

I testified before those committees, and I followed through, and I followed through. And this gives you an idea of how money is being so wildly spent. Many of the Senators and Congressmen said, "You know, you are the best lobbyist for the broadcast media that is here. The NAB are spending millions of dollars, and they are not doing one tenth what you are doing."

Here I was, working just as God provided.

Hill – Yours was a labor of necessity, not one of convenience.

Nicholls – That's right. Another hearing on my bill, Senate Bill Two, was held in one of the largest hearing chambers. The place was packed—two, three, four hundred people. For three days, you had NBC, ABC, and all of these others giving their points of view.

After the third day, before it closed, Senator Pastore blew his stack. And I mean, he blew his stack.

He said, "You people, I don't know what is wrong with you people. I thought you people were intelligent. For three days, all you have done is just go around in circles. You haven't given me one thing I can bite my teeth into. What's wrong with you?"

And then he saw me sitting over in the corner against the wall, and he said, "I see Reverend Nicholls is here. Have you got something to say about this, sir?

I stood to my feet and I said, "Yes, sir."

He said, "Come and say it."

So I went to the microphone, and I said, "Sir, I am the first speaker scheduled for the morning, but that isn't what you asked me about. You wanted to know if I have something to say about why they wasted three days and had nothing to say."

"That's right!" he said. "You got something to say about that?"

"Yes sir," I replied. "Now this has to do with your question about what can we expect from the future. The past usually tells us what we can expect in the future because the past is the best interpreter of the future."

Now, I said, "Sir, the reason they spent three days of your time and didn't give you one single thing to bite your teeth in, is because there isn't a single person here who can authoritatively tell you what the Fairness Doctrine is."

Senator Pastore said, "Oh, I wouldn't say that."

I said, "Well, now listen to me, sir. If there is anybody in this room who knows how *you* define the Fairness Doctrine, I think, sir, you would have to concede that I am that person because I have sat before you longer, and I have heard you expostulate more than any person in this room as to what you believe the Fairness Doctrine is."

Pastore laughed. He says, "Reverend, I will concede this point. You are right."

And then I said, "Sir, I think you will have to concede a second point. Now, if there is anybody in this room who knows how the FCC interprets the Fairness Doctrine (and I pointed to all the chairmen and all the FCC commissioners, they were all there) I think you will have to concede the point that I am the man that knows how these people, the FCC, interpret the Fairness Doctrine."

He started to laugh again, and he said, "You are right. I will concede that second point."

I said, "Sir, that is what has confused me. Now, I know what you say the Fairness Doctrine is. And I know what the FCC says it is. And, sir, you should know there is as much difference between how the FCC interprets the Fairness Doctrine and how you interpret it, as there is difference between day and night."
And he said, "Well, I don't know about that."

"Well, sir, I know. I know how they interpret."

Well, he said, "I will have to agree with you there, that I am sure you are right."

I said, "There was a day, sir when ... if somebody asked me if I knew what the Fairness Doctrine was, yeah, I could tell you. In fact, if you take the Fairness Doctrine and give it to a group of kids in the sixth grade and have them study it and maybe memorize it and you ask them what the Fairness Doctrine is, they would quote it to you.

"But quoting it doesn't really tell you what it is. All it is is words. Every time the FCC makes a decision, you become more and more confused; and, sir, I stand before you today and I tell you, I cannot tell you what the Fairness Doctrine is. And, sir, just to prove my point, I am going to ask in this room (and here you have all the dignitaries of both the Senate and the Senate Committees and of the broadcast world, they were there)—I want somebody to stand to their feet, and come to this microphone, and authoritatively tell us what the Fairness Doctrine is."

I said, "Sir, I will wait (I think it was three minutes) to see if someone can do that. But I am not through yet."

So, we waited. After the allotted time, I said, "Senator Pastore and your committee here, you can see now, there isn't one single person out of these people that can tell you what the Fairness Doctrine is. Let me try this on for size. Do you realize, sir, that I could go on any broadcast station in America, and I could call John Jones a thief, I could call him a scoundrel, I could call him a crook, I could call him a womanizer, I could call him an adulterer, I could call him a fornicator, I could go on and on for a whole half hour, I could castigate his honesty, his integrity, and his other like personal facts, and I wouldn't violate the Fairness Doctrine?"

He says, "Oh, yes you would!"

I said, "No, sir, I wouldn't, and I will tell you why. The reason, sir, because there is no controversial issue of public importance being discussed."

He said, "Well, that's not the way it is supposed to act."

I pointed to the FCC commissioners, and I said, "They are the ones that have made it act that way." I said, "Sir, there was a day and age when evolution was a controversial issue of public importance, and I take you back to the debates of Darrow and [William] Jennings [Bryan]."

I said, "There, evolution was a controversial issue of public importance. I wish, sir, that I could stand before you and honestly say that evolution today is a controversial issue of public importance. I would have to admit, it is a controversial issue, but it is not a controversial issue of public importance. I hope and pray that not too long in the future it will once again become a controversial issue of public importance."

Nicholls - Now, do you follow my point there? That is how the Fairness Doctrine was being used and can be used in that same way today. It will mean anything that any group of people want it to be when they are in power. They can interpret any way they like. I happen to have in my files forty-two of the famed statements that were made by Chuck Colson. Mr. Colson, before his conversion to Christ, was a very ruthless man. He would walk over his grandmother's grave and stomp on it, and wouldn't even have any hesitation or conscience in doing it. I have his forty-some statements that he made, that were "For Eyes Only" and were not to be released outside of a certain area. There he said what they were going to do when the Republican Party got Mr. Birch in as their chairman of the FCC. And who they were going to put the screws to once they controlled the broadcast media.

Nicholls - Now, Kenneth, my position is, we cannot afford to allow either Democrats or the Republicans to have control of the broadcast media. We cannot allow the liberal or socialists, or the so-called conservatives, to control the media. We need full protection of the First Amendment.

Hill – Jim, in thinking about the Fairness Doctrine and the kinds of absolute control and power this gives, this is a bureaucratic nightmare and it reminds you once again of how bureaucracies work, as opposed to how government is supposed to work.

Nicholls – That's right.

Hill – There are continuing attempts, are there not, to reinstate the Fairness Doctrine?

Nicholls – Yes. In the last two sessions of Congress, when the last session of Mr. Reagan was in [office], a bill went through both the House and Senate to reinstate the Fairness Doctrine. And it passed through both the House and the Senate and it was only because Mr. Reagan vetoed the bill that it was stopped. When Mr. Bush was in, again the Fairness Doctrine came up, both before the House and before the Senate, and once again it sailed right through both Houses. But Mr. Bush vetoed the bill. So, it did not become law. Now can you imagine if it goes through both the House and Senate this time, that Mr. Clinton would veto the bill? Who is pushing to get this bill through? This is what disturbs me. It is that same liberal, socialist group that are trying to push and get it through. Why are they pushing and trying to get it through? To me it is nothing more than [that] they could control, once more, the broadcast media.

Hill – I think that we have to think that it is not just the broadcast media in general. It is, in particular, the conservative broadcast media and the God-and-country media, as you would call it. Those that would stand for the truth. Those that would stand for the Bible. Those that would stand for morality. We have heard it called by many names besides just the so-called Fairness Doctrine. The Fairness in Broadcasting Act, and many other things. But when one presents the perspective of a Christian or perspective of truth from Scripture, it becomes controversial very quickly sometimes. That is really what they are going after, isn't it?

Nicholls – That's right.

Hill – We're talking about approximately eleven hundred Christian-formatted broadcast facilities now in this country. There were nowhere near that when you were facing the Fairness Doctrine challenge. Also, we have a rising number of secular talk show radio stations.

Nicholls – I like to believe that the only reason there [are] so many of them now and so many talk shows, is because men like Dr. McIntyre and myself paid the price and fought the battle and fought it to a successful conclusion. We drove the forces of evil back. Now they are rearing their heads again and we are faced with another battle. Now, who is going to fight this battle next time?

Hill – We must involve our listeners. We need to call them to action, much as Carl McIntyre and you did in the past. We must not sit idly by and allow these kinds of intrusions upon the broadcast medium and upon our freedoms to go unchallenged.

Nicholls – The Bible tells us that we are the salt of the earth. We Christians are the preserving influence. And if salt has lost its savor, it is good for nothing but to be trodden under foot of men. And I sometimes wonder as I look at the Christians in America if we are not salt—that the only good use we have is to be trodden under the foot of men. We are afraid to stand up for what is right. We are afraid to take a stand for what the Bible says. We are afraid to stand up and call homosexuality sodomy. That is what it is, and God is opposed to it. It is an abomination in His eyes. We are afraid to take a stand against abortion or against fornication or adultery or Biblical morality. What is this nation going to come to?

Nicholls - Are we going to find [ourselves] in the same position as Holland? I met a pastor when I was in Russia a little over a year ago; this pastor was from Holland. He used to have charge of the Christian broadcast facility in all of the Netherlands. He said, "Nicholls, I hope you can take back to the people of America a lesson that we in Holland learned too late. Do you realize that we preachers in Holland cannot preach against adultery from our pulpits; we cannot preach against fornication. We cannot preach against homosexuality from our pulpits. It is a violation of the law. And the only reason we find ourselves in that position is because we preachers and Christians did not take a strong enough stand before it became law."

Hill – What is the call to action? What can our listener do to protect himself or herself? What can we do to work against these kinds of things, and in particular, the Fairness Doctrine?

Nicholls – First, prayer. Prayer is our most forceful and littlest-used weapon that we have today. We must get back to where we are on praying ground with God. Every church used to have "prayer warriors," and if there was ever a day and age when America needs to bathe its ministry and its position in prayer, that must be today.

Secondly, I believe every Christian needs to contact their Senators and contact their Representative in the House, and there I am referring to basically what they call Congressmen. And tell them under no condition should the Fairness Doctrine ever be passed. If they want to do something good for America, give the broadcasters First Amendment rights. Freedom of the press. A rose is a rose no matter what you call it. The press is the press. People today get most of their news through the electronic press, not through the printed page. Way back in history, in fact as far back as the middle 1800s, people got most of their news in many parts of the country through what they call the "town crier." You remember the town crier in history?

Hill – He was a very loud fellow who had the information.

Nicholls – Yes. Now there used to be some printing presses, but printing presses were very costly and very scarce way back then. So, you even had some handwritten newspapers. But the town crier would go through the streets, and he would cry the news. The broadcast media is the town crier. And the First Amendment would protect the town crier just as much as it would protect the man who printed the press or wrote the news out in longhand. News is news, and nothing should be done to infringe on the freedom of the press. And nothing should be done to destroy the very foundation of our country. It needs [to be] strengthened. And our foundation, I will remind you once more, is built upon God's Holy Word. Every principle of freedom that is in our Constitution is built upon a Biblical foundation. We have got to get back to it.

These interviews were previously published in "Reflections on the Fairness Doctrine," copyright 1994, by Southwest Radio Church.

2007 Interview with Dr. Don Smith, President The Radio Bible Hour

Dr. Kenneth Hill interviewed Dr. Don Smith, President of the Radio Bible Hour and son of the late J. Harold Smith, in late 2007. Following is the full text of that interview.

Hill: Your dad was involved in the history of the "Fairness Doctrine." Tell me about his activities.

Smith: In the early 40's, the ministry moved from South Carolina shortly after the death of my brother. And Dad moved the ministry to Knoxville; and at that time, Knox County was involved in the debate over selling beer and liquor. After Prohibition had been repealed, it was left up to a county-by-county option as to whether liquor would be sold, or whether the counties would remain "dry," as they said in those days.

Dad, of course, felt that the liquor industry was a scourge in the country, and he fought it tooth and nail. It's very much like the legalization-of-marijuana debate that's going on in our own day...he felt like it was better to keep it illegal and that the underground traffic wasn't nearly the threat as making it available to every high school kid with a fake driver license—or in some cases, no identity—to be able to go and buy it in their local stores.

Dad received death threats. The Knoxville News-Sentinel newspaper was very much in favor of the liquor industry. They were expecting to make a lot of money in advertising revenues. Dad went on the radio in Knoxville and began to preach about this issue. It was a public issue, and one that attracted considerable attention.

He was attacked by the media generally, and to make a long story short, Dad had some public demonstrations at the Knoxville News-Sentinel newspaper. And they turned out...estimates ranged between 30,000 and 50,000, or maybe more, and that was the largest crowd that had ever been assembled in Knoxville, Tennessee, to that date. And it continued to be the largest until the Tennessee Vols began to attract larger football crowds than they had in those days.

Now when you start to attract large numbers of people in the streets... who is going to begin to pay attention to that? Well, your politicians took notice very, very quickly—that this radio preacher from South Carolina was able to turn out more people into the streets, more activists, more people who were willing to get up and do something—than they had been able to do.

And word began to filter up the chain of command, I suppose...I'm speculating about what probably happened...but suddenly my Dad found himself the attention, or the object of attention, of the FCC—the Federal Communications Commission—and eventually, the national administration, the Truman administration at that time. And they began to take a look at his involvement in media with the aim, I think, of shutting him up.

It was important to them when a person emerged that might have some political influence, and if they were not of liberal stripe. And in those days, we know now from the records and so forth that have emerged—especially from some of the Russian security agencies, and so forth—that a lot of money was coming from Marxist sources to finance a lot of these political sort of entities that existed in our national government at the time. And my dad was always...post-World War II... a strong anti-communist...and he believed and read the record of communism—that the first thing they may go after in the Soviet Union is the churches, to co-opt them or silence them. And so, my dad really felt that this movement was an attempt...it was an extension...of this evil of Marxism in the world.

And he very quickly learned that he was on the receiving end of some real negative attention from that group, which was strongly entrenched in the national government—the State Department, the FCC, and some of these other national agencies at that time. Now, people at that time said, "Oh, you're just being paranoid about this, you know ... this is our government, you know...they're here to protect us, you know, and help us."

We'd come through World War II and the national government was very popular at that time. It was very strong; it had defeated Nazi Germany. And so, it was a very difficult time to find yourself in opposition to a popular government.

[Before they came after him] he had bought time...he had a contract for time on a Mexican radio station. At that time, it was a very, very large radio station on the border, just across the border from Del Rio, Texas, called XERF. And he, above everything else, gave his life to spreading the Gospel. That was all Dad was interested in. He did not care about the politics. He just wanted to preach the Gospel. And he went into that Mexican station, bought time, gave the money to help develop the station.

And in return for that, they gave him a contract for time. He did not own the station in any way. He simply had a long-term contract for two time slots, early in the morning and 8 o'clock in the evening. And so, the FCC ruled that he owned that station. Now, we buy time on your radio station and we don't...we would never claim that we *own* your station. And so, just on the face of that, it was a silly charge.

But...they had the "guns" to make it stick. And ...at that time, if you owned—if you had a share of ownership—in a foreign station, you could not legally own a U.S.-based station.

Dad had really kind of foreseen the importance of the media, and had gotten the broadcast rights for radio stations in Knoxville, Memphis, and Nashville, including what were then called the proposed television outlet rights for those stations. There was no television at that time. But Dad had seen the first demonstration of television in New York City at the RCA building back in the forties, and felt like this was going to be something that would eventually become an important medium.

So, the FCC ruled that he owned interest in this and they stripped them of the rights to own radio stations in the U.S. Now, that court case went all the way up, and as I understand it, they lost the court case. The courts ruled in favor of the government and said, no, this does constitute ownership and you cannot own these stations.

Basically, in a punitive way, they thought they could shut him up if they threatened him with the court case. They thought he would just sort of quiet down and just go about his business of preaching—and just, you know, give up the attempt to motivate people to influence the votes.

And so, that was kind of his history in there...he had a strong mistrust of the attempt by government in any way to try to get in and influence what people were saying on the radio. He was really a believer in free speech. And what was regarded as offensive in those days were things that, you know, were pretty far out there.

But if you think about what's offensive today...if I get on the radio and preach the fundamental claim of Christianity—that Jesus Christ is the Son of God and that Jesus Christ is the only way to salvation—that's going to be offensive to many people today. That's going to be declared as an offensive, controversial claim and statement.

And so, every person, atheist, individuals of other religions, those who are not Christians—are they then going to have the right to come on and say...in their claim for equal time... that Jesus is not the Son of God and He is not the only way to salvation?

That would have been...I mean it would have been *shocking* to people in the 1940's to think that the government would be involved in some way [today] when they wanted to make the public claim on the radio that Jesus Christ was the Son of God. For them to have even imagined that a Muslim...cleric...would then be allowed by law to come on and tell them that this was not true—that this was blasphemy against Allah, or whatever they wanted to say. I mean...it would not have occurred to them, would it? That would have been so far in the range of fantasy that they would have regarded it as science fiction.

But we have changed. We have given up, piece by piece, our right to freedom of speech; and we have given up, piece by piece, our right to proclaim our faith. And so, the result is today that about the only religion [about which] you can make a television show that ridicules that faith, or demeans that faith, or makes a mockery of the person that believes that faith is divine...the religion you're allowed to do that to... is Christianity...Christians.

You can go and you can get a nice amount of funding from Hollywood to make a movie that ridicules Christians. Or you can get on the radio for hours...or on the television for hours...and you can talk about the corruption in the Church. You can talk about the corruption of the [church] leaders; you can claim that all Catholic priests are perverts and child molesters. And you'll get funds for that. And you'll get support, and you can broadcast that. And you can put that out.

But if you make the claim that Jesus Christ is the exclusive pathway to Heaven or to a relationship with God, that's offensive. That's offensive and you'd better not make a threat against certain religions or they will threaten, at least, to cut your head off! So, you know... we're [regarded as] "militant" Christians. People who simply want to proclaim their faith are equated, on one news network documentary, as being the same as—equivalent to—people who violently kill and blow up children and do these atrocious acts around the world.

And...a person like Jerry Falwell is claimed by this religious media to be the same. "No different from" was the statement. No different from these other people. So we see how far we've come...and I'm delighted that you're working on this topic.

It's a very, very dangerous notion to make this equivalence between the militant, bomb-making expressions of one religion and the free speech of another religion, and say they are the same. I have no problem with a Muslim or a Buddhist or a Hindu, or anybody else, buying time on a radio station and proclaiming their view. Christianity is quite comfortable in an open discussion and an open debate. But what we are not happy with is the idea that we can no longer make claims—that we can no longer preach what we believe is Biblical truth. That is the foundation of our lives.

And we may see a day when we have to make dangerous sacrifices to continue to preach the Gospel of Christ. The Gospel is offensive and it always has been. And the Bible tells us that to some people the Bible is an offense. The Gospel is an offense and an affront.

At the time, Dad was taking [up] a simple moral issue: Is it right for the society to endorse the sale and consumption of alcoholic beverages? Is that a good thing or a bad thing? And we see, probably conservatively, 15- to 20,000 people die a year in automobile accidents from having purchased legally-available alcohol. We see the destruction of marriages and homes.

We see alcohol as the gateway drug for many other kinds of drugs. In our young people, we see enormous numbers of teen pregnancies, abortions which you can trace back to the fact that the kid was drunk when they had sex. I mean...we could just go on, we could list these enormous numbers of social ills that we see that are related to the liquor industry.

And I think my dad was on the right side in that fight. I think he was doing the Lord's work when he was on the radio saying, "Don't go down this road, because if we do, we will pay an enormous price." And I think about the people who stood up against him and fought with him on that...there was a preacher in Knoxville that went to Washington and testified against him and told lie after lie in the FCC hearings...and Dad went on the radio, and (talk about "offensive"!) he said, "This particular man has lied about God's work and God's man in this case."

"And," he said, "the Lord has revealed to me, he's gonna kill him for it." And on the way back from Washington, that pastor got sick; and he got progressively more ill, and he talked about being "offensive" on the radio. Dad would go on the radio every morning in Knoxville and give a health report of this pastor. And the fellow died shortly thereafter. God is not mocked...the truth will be the truth...regardless of what the politicians think about it, or who's "offended" by it. Jesus Christ said, "*I am the Way, the Truth, and the Life.*" He came so that every person could have that new relationship with God. And He came offering that gift of His life so that we could...we could have that.

And Dad simply preached the Gospel. He simply shared truth—the Biblical truth as he saw it—and if we lose the right to do that, we will pay a terrible price, just as we paid a terrible price in this culture for walking down the path of legalization of drugs. Alcohol's a drug. We legalized it, made it socially acceptable, made it something that you didn't have to go and hide in shame to do.

And, again...we see the legislators will face a choice...when they come to make this choice on the "Fairness Doctrine." We have people in this country who hate religion, they hate God, they are enemies of God.

Every once in awhile on the world stage, we'll see the emergence of an organization of evil in the world. And I believe that we saw that in the 1930's with the emergence of Nazi Germany which had a strong anti-Semitic, occult underpinning in that movement. It was a movement of evil.

We saw it in the Soviet Union with the emergence of Marxism and that anti-God doctrine that was introduced there, too: Stop worship and make religion irrelevant. The Soviets under Stalin saw that they couldn't wipe out religion. So their next strategy was just "Let's 'peripheralize' it...let's just make it irrelevant." And so they co-opted the Church in Russia; they put the priests of the Russian Orthodox Church on the payroll. They treated them well, and they made the Church irrelevant.

And, again, I think we see the emergence now on the world stage of this kind of fundamentalism—Islamo-fascism—that seeks to spread its doctrine around the world. Allah is *not* the same god that I worship; and when that movement says that either you have to become a convert to their way of thinking, or become a slave, or die...I don't really like [any] of those three alternatives!

And I think we see that emergence again, on the world stage, of an organized evil. Our enemy is never still; he constantly is at work. And yet you see these same people who are supporting the "Fairness Doctrine" aligning themselves *against* the people who want to fight this Islamo-fascism in the world...you know, they say politics makes strange bedfellows. Evil makes strange bedfellows too.

I think [that] many of these people who are proposing this "Fairness Doctrine" because they ultimately want to silence their political enemies are also trying to silence the voice of Jesus Christ. And they're putting themselves in the company, and in league with, people that they will be sorry that they made an alliance with. It's an alliance of evil that will bear fruit for these people in their lives.

And so, in a sense, we need to be aware that we're facing similar kinds of choices that my Dad faced in the 1940's. He was never ashamed of the choice that he made, and he never saw reason to change his position or apologize for it in the stand that he took. And even though they took away his radio station rights and the television rights—I mean...who knows how much that would have been worth in today's market? But he never regretted that choice...he never regretted doing the right thing.

And I think we just need to encourage our politicians to really think about the moral consequences...who are they really hurting? In the long term, who are they going to be helping with the re-emergence of this "Fairness Doctrine"?

"Termites in the Temple"

Why have paid religious broadcasts
been banned on WNOX?

**A sermon preached to 30,000 people at a protest meeting
Knoxville, Tennessee - Sunday, April 14, 1946
by Rev. J. Harold Smith**
(Published in *The Carolina Watchman* – Vol. 109 – No. 115, May 1946)

I want all my friends to know—as well as my enemies—that this fight on WNOX has not been pleasant or easy. It has been no easy thing to wrestle against powers, against the rulers of the darkness of this world, against spiritual wickedness in high places.

But we feel that we have a cause, a right, a privilege and a glorious freedom at stake. Our liberties are more valuable than life itself. Did our boys not gladly go into the withering machine gun fire at Okinawa, did they not march over the dead bodies of their buddies on the beachhead of Normandy, that we might enjoy the liberties that spell *America* and not *Russia*?

There seems to have been quite a joke made of my subject for the afternoon. Yesterday, Mr. Westergaard, manager of WNOX, said his close friends had started calling him "Termite." I want to assure all of you who are listening to me that I have never thought of Mr. Westergaard or any of the local staff as termites. But I have wondered quite often just what Mr. Jack Howard, owner of said station and the man who is the one who gave the order that all "Paid Religious Programs" be banned from the air lanes of WNOX is. However, the "termites" I want to discuss with you this afternoon are far greater than even Mr. Jack Howard or his father Roy Howard, owner of the *News-Sentinel*.

The Text

Our text is found in the Old Testament in the Book of Ezekiel, chapter 8, verse 7:

> "And he brought me to the door of the court;
> and when I looked, behold a hole in the wall."

> Then verse 8 and 9 declares, "Then said he
> unto me, 'Son of man, dig now in the wall': and
> when I had digged in the wall, behold a door.
>
> Verse 9, "And he said unto me, 'Go in and
> behold the wicked abominations that they
> do here.'"
>
> Verse 10, "And so I went in and saw,
> and behold, every form of creeping
> things and abominable hearts, and all the
> idols of the house of Israel, portrayed upon
> the wall round about."

God's man was allowed to see on the inside. Ezekiel saw the abominations that were working on the inside; and my friends, I declare we need to see the things underneath these strange movements that are now progressing in our city. By the grace of God, I want you to take a peep this afternoon through the "hole in the wall" and "see the wicked abominations that they do here."

I trust that by the grace of God this afternoon, I may, under the leadership of the Holy Ghost, show you dear friends that this subtle, deceitful, undermining, "New Policy" going into effect over WNOX after tomorrow is both Satanic and has been spawned and spewed forth from the mouth of Hell.

I was in Danville, Va., on March 27th when my telephone rang and Mr. O. L. Smith, assistant manager of WNOX called me and said, "Preacher, I have some bad news for you." He said, "Our station has adopted a new policy. After April 14th your contract will be cancelled. We will refund you the money you have paid in advance for your broadcast."

I said, "Mr. Smith, why are you taking the Radio Bible Hour off the air?" That question has never been answered!

In Prayer

I spent that Wednesday night in prayer and God gave me the assurance about 5:00 o'clock Thursday morning, March 28th--that out of this thing, His Name should be glorified and that Satan would receive one of his greatest defeats. I have never, from that hour, doubted that promise.

I believe that through this thing, a "strangle-hold" and a "death-grip" of a terrible octopus that has been slipping his arms about the people of Knoxville will be broken. It is no secret and everyone who knows anything knows that the "*News-Sentinel*," the mother of WNOX, has always fought for everything the churches of this city opposed. It seems there has been no one in Knoxville willing to suffer the smear campaign that this newspaper would wage against the person who called their number. I charge this afternoon that the Knoxville *News-Sentinel* and her affiliated Radio Station WNOX are anti-God, anti-Bible, anti-Church, and anti-Gospel and anti-preacher.

God, the Bible, the church, the Gospel, and every God-called preacher is against liquor. The *News-Sentinel* and WNOX are "dyed in the wool" *for* it. God, the Bible, the Church, the Gospel and every true preacher declares that the "Sabbath is a Holy Day." The *News-Sentinel* is an advocate of defiling it. These statements cannot be challenged.

Now, in their latest attack upon God's preachers, I declare they have struck at the very vitals of our American way of life. They have struck a direct blow at our constitutional rights as freeborn Americans. It was in this old state, down in Dayton, Tennessee, where John T. Scopes said that men came from monkeys. It was down here in old East Tennessee where that devilish theory had its satanic head crushed beneath the heel of William Jennings Bryan. It cost Mr. Bryan his life, but evolution was defeated and none but a few "crack pots" believe such "Tom foolery" today. It was Henry T. Burns, from Tennessee, the Old Volunteer State, who cast the deciding vote giving every woman in this great meeting this afternoon the right to vote. This state has been first in war and first in peace. And, friends, I believe we are assembled this afternoon in one of the greatest protest meetings ever to be held in this state.

Principle Involved

You did not come here this afternoon because J. Harold Smith was involved. You came here because of a principle—a right that you believe in, that I believe in, that every true American believes in—and that is right and justice for all—regardless of whether he be Jew, or Greek, white or black, weak or strong, rich or poor.

If this struggle only involved the few so-called "Racketeering Radio Preachers," I would not waste my time in protesting. I would not have begged you to come to this central meeting place. My friends, I have called you here that we might get a look through the "Hole in the wall" at the "Abominations that they do here."

Shortened version:

I am shocked, yea, even amazed that so soon—even before scores of our returning veterans have found a job or their gaping wounds healed—an attempt [is being] made to take away from us one of the four freedoms, that the late President, Mr. Franklin D. Roosevelt, so faithfully assured us would be our heritage, and that of our children—if we would only sacrifice our husbands and sons and fathers and sweethearts on the battle fields of Europe, and the hot steaming jungles of the faraway Pacific. Was he only kidding us? From the recent action taken by "your *News-Sentinel* Station, WNOX," one would judge that there will have to be another battle for you G.I.'s to fight.

There was a time before the war when your Knoxville *News-Sentinel* Station, WNOX, was very anxious to sell preachers time. Then, she had *no* convictions about taking money away from "poor preachers." Not until two weeks ago did they have this change of heart. They said they had been convicted in this matter—that their conscience hurt them over selling time to preachers. Well, they haven't said anything about giving all the money I have paid them the past five years back to me. If they did, it would be to the tune of about $60,000. I am not complaining about the money I have paid the station. I do not regret it. Just one soul of the thousands who have been saved as a result of this broadcast, and [broadcasts] of the other preachers who have so faithfully declared God's Word—is worth every dollar spent and every tear shed, and every hour of preparing the messages. Just to visit every day [by radio] in the home of cripples, of the aged, of the invalid, of the sinner and the saint was worth it all. My stay in Knoxville and my broadcasting over the *"News-Sentinel"* Station WNOX has been a most pleasant one.

WNOX Grows Rich

I repeat: there was a time before the war when WNOX was in her infancy, when she was little and weak. She needed financial support. The preachers were welcome then with their "shekels;" but now, your *News-Sentinel* Station WNOX has grown into a mighty giant. She is East Tennessee's most powerful radio station. She has grown rich. Last year, she did over $500,000, one-half million dollars worth of business. I repeat: "Your *News-Sentinel* Station WNOX has grown rich off the "blood of your sons." Big business, beer, and cigarettes prospered during the war. They were able to buy more time. That's all right, too. They have the right to buy it if they have the money—*and so do I!*

Your *News-Sentinel* Station WNOX has been blessed. The Bible says that God blessed Pharaoh for Joseph, his servant's sake. Your *News-Sentinel* Station WNOX, up until two weeks ago, was friendly toward the Gospel. They sold to all alike. But orders came down from an "absentee owner" who lives in New York City, saying "Get all those 'Hill-Billy' preachers off my *News-Sentinel* Station WNOX by April 15th. I had thought, up until then, it was *"your"* *News-Sentinel* Station;" but now I have learned that it is Mr. Jack Howard's, of 230 Park Avenue, New York City, New York. They say they have to "ban" us preachers. That's right! They haven't banned us, they have "canned" us.

I have not fought the owners of the *"News-Sentinel* Station WNOX"* because they are giving "free time" to the churches and preachers. The *News-Sentinel* Station (you will notice I am leaving off the word "your") has in years past given me one hour and 55 minutes a year "free time."

They always carried my "New Year's" all-night service for one hour and 45 minutes. I had no objections to this; in fact, I appreciated it. That is *not* the *issue*! The *News-Sentinel* Station would like for you folk to believe that I am selfish and want to "bag-up" all the time. That isn't true. I am convinced that "Contributed time is controlled time." I don't care for that kind of time over any man's radio station!

"New Policy"

When the *News-Sentinel* Station WNOX first adopted this "New Policy," they were going to contribute to the "poor preachers" of East Tennessee two choice hours a week out of their 140 broadcasting hours. They were also going to give to their listening audience many wonderful talks and spiritual speeches. Of course, when I began to ridicule this set-up, they jumped their "religious diet" [that] they are going to cram down your throats, up to 5 ½ hours. Well, some of these preachers that are raising so much sand about me protesting this thing will have me to thank for three hours and a half more each week. Now, that should make some of you preachers happy. At least, I got something accomplished for you. Don't worry. It won't last long. If I don't miss my guess, the *News-Sentinel* Station WNOX is fixing to "crucify some preachers."

You say, "Mr. Smith how many times were you offered free time over the *News-Sentinel* Station WNOX?" Three times. "How many times did you refuse it?" Three times. "Will you ever use any of their "free time"? Never, as long as they have their present "New Policy."

Now here is the question. Do I have the right—or any other preacher who can produce the money—to purchase time at their regular commercial rates to broadcast the Gospel? I am an American, President of the Southern Bible Institute, publisher of the *Carolina Watchman*, publisher of a songbook and a licensed and ordained missionary Baptist preacher. Why can't I buy time? That is the question the *News-Sentinel* WNOX has never answered. Is my money different from "Kay's Ice Cream" or "Fowler Brothers' Furniture?" You know it isn't. Then why won't they sell me time? There is a reason! Maybe they want to put something on at my hour as "silly"—as when they substituted the "*News-Sentinel*'s Sunday Funnies" for Major Boswell's program. Now wasn't that "smart" on the part of the station!

I believe that God permitted that to happen to show you people here in Knoxville that the devil wants to substitute FABLES and FUNNIES for the Gospel! Friends, that would be funny if it weren't so tragic. Major Boswell had been on the *News-Sentinel* Station WNOX for eight years, trying to reach the prisoners; but now, your *News-Sentinel* Station is going to cram down the innocent throats of your children on God's day the "Silly Funnies." Do you see what the *News-Sentinel* wants? At the masthead of their paper, they should carry, "Funnies, movies, liquor."

"All (?) Can Advertise"

Yes, friends, every one can advertise over the *News-Sentinel* Station WNOX—except preachers! Why, they advertise ice cream, cigarettes and candy. They advertise chewing gum, furniture, automobiles, soft drinks, headache pills, and "Rooster Snuff." They sell time to *Life Magazine*, *True Story*, *Saturday Evening Post*; and ever so often you hear them put in one of these little "ditties":

> "Tick-Tock, Ten o'clock,
> Tick-Tock, Two o'clock,
> Tic-Tock, Four o'clock,
> Time to stop and get a cold 'Doc'
> When you're hungry, thirsty and tired."

Or maybe it's:

> "Pepsi-Cola hits the spot,
> Twelve full ounces that's a lot,
> Twice as much for a nickel too,
> Pepsi-Cola is the drink for you."

Now, friends, I have nothing against these companies. Right now, in fact, a good Pepsi would be O.K., and as thirsty as I am, a Dr. Pepper would hit the spot. But if all these things can come over your radio, why should I be kept from saying, "For God so loved the world that he gave his only begotten Son that whosoever believeth on him should not perish but have everlasting life."

I have yet to be shown I don't have that right. Someone besides Mr. Jack Howard, owner of the *News-Sentinel* Station will have to tell me I don't have that right before I will believe it.

I further contend that if the program I put on the air is one that serves the "public interest, convenience, and "necessity" then I have a right to be heard. Mr. Jack Howard, neither [does] the Knoxville *News-Sentinel* own the air waves. They belong to the people, and are only loaned by our government to him. If he misuses them then they may be taken away. It would indeed be said, should the people of this section rise up in such a mighty and indignant protest, that F.C.C. should take away the license of said station. It is not at all impossible for such a thing to be done.

"Absentee Ownership"

You ask me, what is the reason for the *News-Sentinel* Station refusing preachers, churches, and religious organizations the privilege of purchasing time. Here is the basic fundamental reason. It is not because they think we preachers are getting rich out of the matter, but because of their hate for the things of God. I say at the very bottom of all this is Satan. He is responsible for this dastardly deed. We would have already had the "Old Policy" restored, but the "absentee ownership" of the *News-Sentinel* Station, WNOX, says you folks of East Tennessee are not capable of choosing what is good for your listening ear. You must get out of this business of listening to these "Hill-billy" preachers and let us give you some "wonderful speeches."

O.K., friends, beginning tomorrow you will have them. I wonder if they will be as silly as the wonderful speeches that followed Major Boswell's program and Hoyt Shaddon. Mr. Howard says, "We want to give you some free preaching. We know you are tired of hearing these 'radio shysters, racketeers and hoodlums'. We feel so sorry they have been taking you poor folks' money."

What about the beer? Does it get the man's money? Friends, this argument will *not* hold water!

They say they have had a change of heart and no longer want to take a preacher's money. Folks, do you believe that? Well, the Station realized she wasn't doing so well in making you folk believe their "pitiful tales," so they call upon their Star Editor up at the Knoxville *News-Sentinel* to jump [on] these "racketeering Radio Preachers." So on Friday night past, he comes out with his masterpiece under the [title], "No Price On Religion."

Now folks, I am sure Mr. Editor thought, "This will certainly give the folk of Knoxville and of East Tennessee the (information they need). They will surely believe me. Since I am working so hard to get Sunday movies and liquor (when they vote in the referendum on August first) I know they will believe my article."

As soon as I read that editorial I said to my wife, "That will cost Mr. Roy Howard's Knoxville *News-Sentinel* five thousand subscribers." I have moved my sights up. I believe there will be ten thousand people in Knoxville and East Tennessee who will never permit another "*News-Sentinel*" paper to be left on their doorstep. My subscription stopped today. Since I came to Knoxville five years ago, I have read the pages of this newspaper, but it has become so openly opposed to what God's people love in this city [that] I feel every time I pick up that newspaper I need a bath in Lysol!

[The] very heading of the article ["No Price on Religion"] is false. You are not your own [i.e., you have been bought with the price of the blood of Jesus Christ]. In 1 Peter 1:18 and 19 we read: "Forasmuch as ye know that ye were not redeemed with corruptible things, as silver and gold, from your vain conversation received by tradition from your fathers;

But with the precious blood of Christ, as of a lamb without blemish and without spot:"

"Stroke Stage"

The first section of this article states (quote), "Certain radio preachers are attempting to pump up the community's blood pressure because two of the local radio stations have decided to stop selling time to them" (end quote). It seems to me that there are certain radio stations and a certain newspaper by the name of *News-Sentinel* whose blood pressure is up. In fact, friends, they are near the "stroke stage." I wouldn't be surprised if in six months they will be buried and forgotten. I have received hundreds of letters saying the *News-Sentinel* is out of their home to stay. I know of at least one friend who cancelled his year's contract of advertising with them. I know of hundreds who are telling their "paper boys" to stop their paper. Several of the paperboys are planning to quit. Now, whose blood pressure is up?

Who knows, maybe the Editor and writer of this article, "No Price On Religion" may have to leave his editorial desk and start delivering his own papers. Reckon these "cancellations" and stops" will make the blood pressure of Mr. Roy Howard, the father of Jack Howard, the Czar of Radio Station WNOX go up? Keep watching the "Want Ads" department in the *Knoxville Journal*. I'm sure that's the paper Knoxvillians will soon be reading—for a "position wanted" [ad] by the editor and composer of "No Price On Religion."

In said article, this gentleman goes on to say (quote), "It is not our (*The News-Sentinel*) business to defend the policy of a radio station; in fact, contrary to some impressions, this newspaper owns and controls no radio station, although WNOX and the *News-Sentinel* do observe a "Mutual Promotional Agreement" (end quote).

"Mutual Promotional Agreement"

Now, friends, I wonder if the editor of the *News-Sentinel* thought the intelligent people of Knoxville would believe that. On the hour, every hour, the announcer says, "This is your *News-Sentinel* Station." The *News-Sentinel* article "No Price On Religion" states (quote), "WNOX and the *News-Sentinel* do observe a mutual promotional agreement" (end quote), I am sure none of us will deny this. They *do* have a mutual agreement to "bring liquor" to our city. Habakkuk 2:15, "Woe unto him that giveth his neighbor drink." We know that the *News Sentinel* has always advocated the "Open Liquor Store." Legalized liquor, Sunday movies and anything to drag down and destroy the sacredness of our faith and the church of the Lord Jesus Christ.

If there is anything God's Word deals with in no uncertain tones, it is the "Liquor Question" and His blessed and Holy Day. So from this article we gather that WNOX has a "Mutual promotional agreement" to put across the Sunday movies and the legalized liquor, August 1st. One of the big hindrances to such a godless "mutual promotional agreement" is to get the preachers who fight such "mutual promotional agreements" off the air.

"Mr. Editor" of the Knoxville *News-Sentinel* goes on to say (quote), "From what we understand about the matter, WNOX and WROL have taken a commendable stop toward program improvement" (end quote). From this statement all of you see the *News-Sentinel* is still carrying out their "mutual promotional agreement" to get rid of all the preachers they could not dominate. Before I will become a little soft-soaping, pussy-footing, back-scratching, ear-tickling, time-begging, sin-dodging, excuse-making, editor-covered preacher [used] to camouflage the programs of the Knoxville *News-Sentinel* and her child WNOX, I'll just keep on preaching from "Truck platforms."

"Price Tags"

Our beloved Editor of the Knoxville *News-Sentinel* goes on to say (quote), "in effect, the decision removed the 'price tag' from religion" (end quote). Well, since when did this said editor become so interested in "price tags"? We have never argued with the station officials at WNOX about the "price tags." You friends, who for five years have never failed to support these religious programs, have never worried about these "price tags." Maybe it is the Editor's "high blood pressure" that is causing him to worry about these price tags. I don't know the editor of the *News-Sentinel*, writer of "No Price On Religion," but I am sure I could take twenty-five cents and pay him off in full for all he has ever donated to any religious program that had for its purpose the winning of lost souls to God. Those who always holler about the "cost" and the "money" of said programs are generally the tight wads, skinflints, nickel nibblers, and penny-pinchers of your community. You're welcome!

He further states (quote), "We suppose this policy has long been in effect elsewhere in the country, and that it has the approval of the Federal Communications Commission" (end quote). Yes, I am sorry to add that "this policy" has "long been" in effect in countries [such as] Italy, Japan, Germany, and Russia. Every radio station the Scripps-Howard, Inc, gets their hands on soon falls under the axe. Believe me, friends, when I tell you that the Termite of Communism is gnawing the "mud-sills" of our Christian foundations from beneath us. If we are to attach importance to latest reports, Russia is definitely out to conquer the world.

From an inside source at Washington, I can tell you what Russia is driving toward as her major objectives for the immediate future. Russia wants complete control of the nations on all sides of her gigantic borders. She wants a warm water port on the Persian Gulf. She wants the oil fields of Iran. She wants everything around the Black Sea, including Turkey. She wants to cut the British lifeline through the Mediterranean. She wants to break up the British Empire.

These are only her first objectives. Then, she expects to bring the U.S. under her heel. Russia wants a "Red World," with the entire human race under the slavery of Moscow. Christians, I shudder to think what such a world would mean for us. May God help Knoxville to "wake up" before it is too late.

Do you know the one thing that stands in Moscow's way more than anything else? I will tell you: *It is the children of God*, regardless of denominational affiliations or race. God's saints stand as the great force opposing this termite. Communism is anti-God, anti-Christ, and anti-Church. Christians are pro-God, pro-Christ, pro-Church. Joseph Stalin knows that the loyal followers of Christ must be silenced in America in order to "put over" his program.

Smear Campaign

Orders have gone out from Moscow to knock down the leaders—the Gospel Preachers. God have mercy on any preacher of any faith who will join in with this godless gang to put across their Hellish program. Friends, I know I am under the "Russian Hammer." My "doom" is sealed, so far as that dirty, yellow-bellied crowd of cowards is concerned; but as long as God wills, I shall continue to fight them with all my soul.

I am in receipt of a letter dated March 23, 1946, from my friend and brother preacher, Harvey H. Springer, Pastor of the Englewood Baptist Tabernacle, Denver, Colorado. From his letter I quote:

> "I can't begin to tell you the unspeakably vicious things that have been done against us (speaking of his church). They started with a smear campaign in the *Rocky Mountain News*, which is a Scripps-Howard newspaper published in Denver. For days they smeared me, my friends, my co-workers, and my church members.

> "But it was not until Sunday night, March 3rd, at the close of a great evangelistic service in our church that the Communists came into the open, acting like the atheists in Russia who have stabbed the cause of Christ to death.

> "By quick action in calling the police, we averted what might have been a bad riot. Because I would not let them put out literature inside our church, published by the Communist Party of Colorado, they had me arrested on charges of assault

and battery. Two rioters were in turn arrested for molesting a religious service. One of the men is a member of the Communist party of the state of Colorado.

"They are getting mighty daring when they come into the church to start trouble, and we simply will not stand for it" (end quote).

On Friday, March 8, 1946, Upton Close, reporting this incident said (quote), "But whatever these persons who met on Denver University campus may have against Rev. Springer, they should be restrained by our American laws and habits from attacking those who come to worship in an American church."

Walter Winchell

The University authorities recognized that something was wrong—but made their own position worse by sending a representative (or so he claimed to be) to disavow what the group was to do. Kurt Singer, author of one of Walter Winchell's (I like to pronounce that name *winch-Hell*) "plug" books—and who was recently entertained, I hear, in the homes of certain Scripps-Howard press editors and special writers—was introduced as [associated with] the "anti-Fascist underground" in Europe, including Norway. Here are stenographic notes taken on his address:

The mysterious Kurt Singer said:

"Friends, somehow I feel at home. I remember similar meetings in Oslo. These meetings were underground and illegal."

"I believe in the liquidation of these American Quislings (**Editor's note**: *Quislings were politicians who collaborated with the Nazis during World War II*) in time."

"We of the underground have our ways of working against these.

One way is to strike them from the paid religious broadcasts."

"The so-called *Reverend* Springer cannot stop you. Why can't we take the numbers of the license plates that belong to people attending his services—they are only little people, owners of grocery stores and barber shops. They are afraid of losing their business. They will understand that! You should publish each week the license numbers of the automobiles. It is very legal!"

"Some of the outstanding "Quisling" Preachers, especially radio preachers who
have paid religious programs, can be called by telephone at two or three o'clock in the morning. Then, you could send these people who attend Springer's church a Nazi Iron Cross and remind them that they are members of the Nazi International."

Scripps-Howard's Friend

Friends, believe me when I tell you this Kurt Singer comes from the "Underground" gutters of Europe! This is the friend entertained in the homes of certain "Scripps-Howard" editors and special writers. Is it from this Kurt Singer [that] Jack Howard, owner of WNOX, got the idea of striking down the "Paid Religious Broadcasts"?

This is one time, and one place where Mr. Kurt Singer's ideas didn't go across! Some of you, I am sure, are now beginning to see why Mr. Editor's statement that "This policy has long been in effect elsewhere" is actually a *fact*.

His statement that such a policy has the approval of the Federal Communications Commission certainly betrays such words as "public interest, convenience, and necessity." Maybe there has been a change in the meaning of the English language since I finished school.

I ask you: when 44,500 letters and protests pour into my office in eleven days ...thousands of other letters go to WNOX and to Mr. Howard, 230 Park Avenue, New York City, New York ... and to our Congressmen, Senators, and the Federal Communications Commission in Washington ...and hundreds of protests pour into the station by telephone—*is it serving the "public interest, convenience, and necessity"?*

Maybe words are like contracts, they don't mean anything anymore. Radio contracts, school board contracts—and by the way, the school board didn't exactly "cancel" my contract—they just called me up and apologized in a nice way for not being able to figure out any way whereby 15,000 people could possibly squeeze into their auditorium unless they overflowed into all the school rooms, basement, etc.

Mr. Adcock said he had just received a letter from Mr. Prince stating that such a thing was just impossible. Mr. Adcock said, "Now, preacher, we will be glad to get together and see what can be done." Maybe if I had met with them we could have raised the roof and put in fifty "balconies." Well, the *News-Sentinel* has made much of my "canceling" the contract!

Well, all of you know when a party rents a building, pays for it, and the agent for the building receives the money—if the contract is broken by the party doing the renting, he forfeits his money. Well, here is the check, returned to me by Mr. Adcock. I leave it to you: *who wanted the contract broken?*

"Mimeographed Letters"

The editor and writer of "No Price On Religion" goes on to say (quote), "Mimeographed letters of protests have been scattered throughout the community, with a blank space for a signature, in efforts to maintain what must be a lucrative business."

I invite the editor to my office to examine 44,500 letters you [people] have written. As to the "lucrative business" we radio preachers have, why didn't Mr. Editor of the *News-Sentinel* get into it? It is not until tomorrow that WNOX puts into effect her new policy. Maybe he can [get into it] by that time! Before this thing is over he may have to use some of this free time. He knows he is lying. You [know], folks—if a preacher dresses half decent, lives in a decent home, [and] drives a nice automobile, these licentious louses, God-haters, liquor promoters begin to cry, "He is a racketeer!" "Out for money!"

Do you know any preacher anywhere that draws down the salary equal to one of the liquor officials of Louisville, Kentucky? Can WNOX and the *News-Sentinel* and their editor—who is working so hard with certain groups in this city to bring liquor to Knoxville—show me any preacher who lives higher, wears finer clothes and drives bigger automobiles than the owners of WNOX and the *News-Sentinel*? The editor of the Knoxville *News-Sentinel* [and] the management of Radio Station WNOX know we preachers are not preaching over their station for the "shekels"—but for precious souls that are lost. When their spiritual eyes are opened they will see this. I stand before God judged in this matter.

I am in receipt of a letter from a dear brother preacher, Rev. D.B Eastep, pastor of Calvary Baptist Church in Covington, Kentucky, dated April 5, 1946. I quote from the letter: "This letter is to inform you that after six years of broadcasting over WCTO at Cincinnati, Ohio, we have been taken off this station. This is not the cause of any preference of ours. We believe that it is directly or indirectly the cause of the Federal Council of Churches."

Friends, this is another termite in the temple. This termite is as filthy as the first, Communism. Brother Eastep went on to say, "The time which we and other fundamental churches used and paid for over this station is now being given free to three 'representative' groups, one of which is the Federal Council of Churches."

Ask your pastor—does his church belong to the Federal Council? And if it does, get out of that church—*fast*. Flee it like you would a den of rattlesnakes! This organization is from Hell! It is a wolf in sheep's clothing. It is a green-eyed monster devouring the faith. I repeat: the

Federal Council of Churches is from Hell!

This station WCTO at Cincinnati, Ohio, is owned by Mr. Jack Howard of the Scripps-Howard, Inc. This one thing ought to show you that it is not the local management, Mr. Westergaard and his staff of workers at WNOX. This thing comes from the "absentee owner"—the big shots in New York City. I know it to be a fact that certain groups are bringing pressure on owners of radio stations to take off the "successful radio preacher" and put on the air these "quack doctors, dumb dogs who cannot bark, pussy-footing, back scratching, ear tickling, show-going, liquor sipping, God-hating, compromising failures who the station has to give free time because they can't pay their own way!

I have never known a Federal Council-compromising "modernist" who could make a go on the radio. I have too much godly pride, and the Gospel I preach is too precious to take from the rich man's (Mr. Howard's) table the few measly crumbs of time he has offered the preachers. At first he only offered two measly hours out of 140 hours. Then, when the loud cry went up from the people, they jumped this up to five and a half hours. Where will they find enough preachers to consume this time? I have no objection to WNOX giving these five and a half hours to the local preachers and churches. That is their business. I will always believe that "contributed time is controlled time." I prefer taking my preaching orders from Heaven and not the "Editorial Room" of the *News-Sentinel* and Mr. Howard's office at 230 Park Avenue, New York City, New York.

Rules Of Life

I tell you, WNOX and the *News-Sentinel* are these days being taught the rules of life. They have much to learn about Americanism [and] about the power of prayer.

I wouldn't have all the prayers going up against *me* that are going up against WNOX and this godless newspaper that has no respect for sobriety, but would make drunkards out of your sons and prostitutes out of your daughters with her open declaration against God's Holy law "of keeping the Sabbath day Holy" and in her hellish efforts to bring to our fair city the cursed "Liquor Store." I have been living in Knoxville five years and didn't know until recently that our city was infested with "gangsters" until certain people began to recognize them on our city streets. How did they know them? [Explanatory Note: "Gangsters" was the derogatory term used by the Knoxville *News-Sentinel* to describe preachers of the Gospel such as Dr. Smith.]

Yes, I repeat: WNOX and the Knoxville *News-Sentinel* need to learn about the precision and efficiency with which Christians operate when stirred—about the attitudes of Americans in East Tennessee, the Old Volunteer State, where men are men. Yes, I repeat: about their attitude toward atheistic, alien, anti-Christ, anti-Bible, anti-Church Communism!

I charge that in this "new policy" adopted by WNOX they are striking a death blow to one of the most blessed of our freedoms—that of worshipping God according to the dictates of our own hearts, and that of free speech. I charge that this "new policy" put every advertiser at the mercy of these would-be dictators. Someone has said, "Give the Devil enough rope and he will hang himself." I believe if WNOX insists on keeping in force her "New Policy" and the *News-Sentinel* continues its anti-God, anti-Church, anti-Bible, and anti-preacher attacks, "that we are witnessing a double hanging here this afternoon."

This third termite gnawing at the mudsills of our American way of life is that of the liquor traffic. God is against liquor. The *News-Sentinel* and WNOX are for it. The word of God is against liquor. The *News-Sentinel* and WNOX advocate it. The church is against liquor. WNOX and the *News-Sentinel* are for it. Every God-called, God-commissioned and God-sent preacher is against it. WNOX and the *News-Sentinel* are trying to bring it back. Every sober, God-fearing, born-again believer is against it. WNOX and the *News-Sentinel* are for it. I understand the beer advertisers have threatened to take their beer spots off the airwaves unless WNOX gets rid of me. Well, the "Beer Dealers" have had their day. God's judgment is surely coming on them.

Think of the broken homes, broken lives, broken hearts, liquor has caused. Think of the sad-eyed mothers, the pale, sick, nervous wives liquor has caused. Think of the little hungry, orphaned children liquor has caused. I want to go on record before all of you as being against liquor whether it is bootlegged or sold in a legalized liquor store. I want to go on record as being on the opposite side of those who advocate its sale and advertise its products.

Conclusion

I close my message by declaring that WNOX and the *News-Sentinel* have lifted their hands against God's anointed. May God have mercy upon them. I further state that I have no ill will in my heart toward the local management, Mr. Westergaard, and Mr. Smith, or the local staff of WNOX. I feel that this matter is greater than any one person or personalities. There are precious blood-bought principles at stake.

Our boys fought, they waded through Hell on earth, they gave up home and loved ones that this American privilege might be ours. I declare that by the grace of God, the *News-Sentinel* and WNOX shall not destroy these blessed principles.

I pray that by the grace of God this "New Policy" may not prevail, but may His Word prevail and the cause of Christ this day march on to one of the greatest Christian victories of our generation.

We will now form in our parade march on WNOX. This parade, I am sure, will be in the Spirit of Christ. I know it will be orderly, and any misconduct will count only for our enemy. This march will be for the glory of God. When we reach the station, there will be a prayer and then our parade will proceed to the old "Mother Bear's Den," The Knoxville *News-Sentinel*. WNOX is only the "Little Cub Bear." Another prayer, and you will be dismissed. As you march, pray.

A Revealing Look at The National Council of Churches

(Formerly, the Federal Council of Churches)

"Few Christian conferences have so struck the hearts and imaginations of churchmen everywhere as did the Malvern Conference of the Church of England, with its bold blueprint for a just and Christian post-war society."

—*TIME Magazine*, Jan. 20, 1941

A little over a year after the Malvern Conference of the Church of England, the "American Malvern" was convened at Ohio Wesleyan University in the United States by the Federal Council of Churches to formulate its own program for a "just and durable peace." *Time magazine* reported on that conference.

AMERICAN MALVERN
TIME – The Weekly Newsmagazine
March 16, 1942

These are the high spots of organized U.S. Protestantism's super-protestant new program for a just and durable peace after World War II:

- Ultimately, "a world government of delegated powers."

- Complete abandonment of U.S. isolationism.

- Strong immediate limitations on national sovereignty.

- International control of all armies and navies.

- "A universal system of money . . . so planned as to prevent inflation and deflation."

- Worldwide freedom of immigration.

- Progressive elimination of all tariff and quota restrictions on world trade.

- "Autonomy for all subject and colonial peoples" (with much better treatment for Negroes in the U.S.).

- "No punitive reparations, no humiliating decrees of war guilt, no arbitrary dismemberment of nations."

- A "democratically controlled" international bank "to make development capital available in all parts of the world without the predatory and imperialistic after-math so characteristic of large-scale private and governmental loans."

This program was adopted last week by 375 appointed representatives of 30-odd denominations called together at Ohio Wesleyan University by the Federal Council of Churches. Every local Protestant chuck in the country will now be urged to get behind the program. "As Christian citizens," its sponsors affirmed, "we must seek to translate our beliefs into practical realities and to create a public opinion which will insure that the United States shall play its full and essential part in the creation of a moral way of international living."

Among the 375 delegates who drafted the program were 15 bishops of five denominations, seven seminary heads (including Yale, Chicago, Princeton, Colgate-Rochester), eight college and university presidents (including Princeton's Harold W. Dodds), practically all the ranking officials of the Federal Council and a group of well-known laymen, including John R. Mott, Irving Fisher and Harvey S. Firestone, Jr. "Intellectually," said Methodist Bishop Ivan Lee Holt of Texas, "this is the most distinguished American church gathering I have seen in 30 years of conference-going."

The meeting showed its temper early by passing a set of 13 "requisite principles for peace" submitted by Chairman [John] Foster Dulles and his inter-church Commission to Study the Bases of a Just and Durable Peace. These principles, far from putting all the onus on Germany or Japan bade the U.S. give thought to the shortsighted selfishness of its own policies after World War I, declared that the U.S. would have to turn over a new leaf if the world is to enjoy lasting peace.

Excerpts:

"For at least a generation we have held preponderant economic power in the world, and with it the capacity to influence decisively the shaping of world events. It should be a matter of shame and humiliation to us that actually the influences shaping the world have largely been irresponsible forces. Our own positive influence has been impaired because of concentration on self and on our short-range material gains. . . . If the future is to be other than a repetition of the past, the U.S. must accept the responsibility for constructive action commensurate with its power an opportunity."

"The natural wealth of the world is not evenly distributed. Accordingly the possession of such natural resources . . . is a trust to be discharged in the general interest. This calls for more than an offer to sell to all on equal terms. Such an offer may be a futile gesture unless those in need can, through the selling of their own goals and services, acquire the means of buying."

With these principles accepted, the conference split up into four groups to study, respectively, the social, economic and political problems of the post-war world and the problem of the church's own position in that world. Discussion waxed hot and heavy, with one notable silence: in a week when the Japs were taking Java, discussion of the war itself was practically taboo. Reason: The Federal Council felt that, since five of its other commissions are directly connected with the war effort, the conference's concern should be with plans for peace.

One war statement -- "The Christian Church as such is not at war"—was proposed by Editor Charles Clayton Morrison, of the influential and isolationist-before-Pearl-Harbor Christian Century. This statement was actually inserted in a subcommittee report by a 64-58 vote after a sharp debate. In the plenary session, however, it was ruled out of order.

Some of the conference's economic opinions were almost as sensational as the extreme Internationalism of its political program. It held that "a new order of economic life is both imminent and imperative"—a new order that is sure to come either "through voluntary cooperation within the framework of democracy or through explosive political revolution."

Without condemning the profit motive as such, it denounced various defects in the profit system for breeding war, demagogues and dictators, "mass unemployment, widespread dispossession from homes and farms, destitution, lack of opportunity for youth and of security for old age." Instead, "the church must demand economic arrangements measured by human welfare . . . must appeal to the Christian motive of human service as paramount to personal gain or governmental coercion."

"Collectivism is coming, whether we like it or not," the delegates were told by no less a churchman than England's Dr. William Paton, co-secretary of the World Council of Churches, but the conference did not vote as far to the left as its definitely pinko British counterpart, the now famous Malvern Conference (Time, Jan. 20, 1941).

It did, however, back up Labor's demand for an increasing share in industrial management. It echoed Labor's shibboleth that the denial of collective bargaining "reduces labor to a commodity." It urged taxation designed "to the end that our wealth may be more equitably distributed." It urged experimentation with government and cooperative ownership.

"Every individual," the conference declared, "has the right to full time educational opportunities . . . to economic security in retirement . . . to adequate health service (and an) obligation to work in some socially necessary service."

The conference statement on the political bases of a just and durable peace proclaimed that the first post-war duty of the church "will be the achievement of a just peace settlement with due regard to the welfare of all the nations, the vanquished, the overrun and the victors alike."

In contrast to the blockade of Germany after World War I, it called for immediate provision of food and other essentials after the war for every country needing them. " We must get back," explained Methodist Bishop Francis J. McConnell, "to a stable material prosperity not only to strengthen men's bodies but to strengthen their souls."

Politically, the conference's most important assertion was that many duties now performed by local and national governments "can now be effectively carried out only by international authority."

Individual nations, it declared, must give up their armed forces "except for preservation of domestic order" and allow the world to be policed by an international army and navy. This League-of-Nations-with-teeth would also have "the power of final judgment in controversies between nations . . . the regulation of international trade and population movements among nations."

The ultimate goal: "a duly constituted world government of delegated powers; an international legislative body, an international court with adequate jurisdiction, international administrative bodies with necessary powers, and adequate international police forces and provision for enforcing its worldwide economic authority."

APPENDIX

V

Rep. Hinchey's

Proposed Legislation for the

Return of the "Fairness Doctrine"

Reintroduced As The
Media Ownership Reform Act (MORA)

From the official website of Rep. Maurice Hinchey (D-NY)
http://www.house.gov/hinchey:

The Media Ownership Reform Act seeks to restore integrity and diversity to America's media system by lowering the number of media outlets that one company is permitted to own in a single market. The bill also reinstates the Fairness Doctrine to protect fairness and accuracy in journalism.

MEDIA OWNERSHIP REFORM ACT

Bill Summary
I. Guarantees Fairness in Broadcasting

Our airwaves are a precious and limited commodity that belongs to the general public. As such, they are regulated by the government. From 1949 to 1987, a keystone of this regulation was the Fairness Doctrine, an assurance that the American audience would be guaranteed sufficiently robust debate on controversial and pressing issues. Despite numerous instances of support from the U.S. Supreme Court, President Reagan's FCC eliminated the Fairness Doctrine in 1987, and a subsequent bill passed by Congress to place the doctrine into federal law was then vetoed by Reagan.

MORA would amend the 1934 Communications Act to restore the Fairness Doctrine and explicitly require broadcast licensees to provide a reasonable opportunity for the discussion of conflicting views on issues of public importance.

II. Restores Broadcast Ownership Limitations

Nearly 60 years ago, the Supreme Court declared that "the widest possible dissemination of information from diverse and antagonistic sources is essential to the welfare of the public, that a free press is essential to the condition of a free society." And yet, today, a mere five companies own the broadcast networks, 90 percent of the top 50 cable networks, produce three-quarters of all prime time programming, and control 70 percent of the prime time television market share. One-third of America's independently-owned television stations have vanished since 1975.

There has also been a severe decline in the number of minority-owned broadcast stations; minorities own a mere four percent of stations today.

- MORA would restore a standard to prevent any one company from owning broadcast stations that reach more than 35 percent of U.S. television households.
- The legislation would re-establish a national radio ownership cap to keep a single company from owning more than five percent of our nation's total number of AM and FM stations.
- The bill would reduce local radio ownership caps to limit a single company from owning more than a certain number of stations within a certain broadcast market, with the limit varying depending upon the size of each market.
- Furthermore, the legislation would restore the Broadcast-Cable and Broadcast-Satellite Cross-Ownership Rules to keep a company from having conflicting ownerships in a cable company and/or a satellite carrier and a broadcast station offering service in the same market.
- Finally, MORA would prevent media owners from grandfathering their current arrangement into the new system, requiring parties to divest in order to comply with these new limitations within one year.

III. Invalidates Media Ownership Deregulation

MORA would invalidate the considerably weakened media ownership rules that were adopted by the Federal Communications Commission in 2003; rules that are now under new scrutiny through the FCC's Future

Notice of Proposed Rulemaking. The legislation further prevents the FCC from including media ownership rules in future undertakings of the commission's Biennial Review Process.

IV. Establishes a New Media Ownership Review Process

MORA creates a new review process, to be carried by the FCC every three years, on how the commission's regulations on media ownership promote and protect localism, competition, diversity of voices, diversity of ownership, children's programming, small and local broadcasters, and technological advancement. The bill requires the FCC to report to Congress on its findings.

V. Requires Reports for Public Interest

MORA requires broadcast licensees to publish a report every two years on how the station is serving the public interest. The legislation also requires licensees to hold at least two community public hearings per year to determine local needs and interests.

H.R.3302

Title: To amend the Communications Act of 1934 to prevent excessive concentration of ownership of the nation's media outlets, to restore fairness in broadcasting, and to foster and promote localism, diversity, and competition in the media.

Sponsor: Rep Hinchey, Maurice D. [NY-22]

Cosponsors (16)
Rep DeFazio, Peter A. [OR-4]
Rep Filner, Bob [CA-51]
Rep Hastings, Alcee L. [FL-23]
Rep Kaptur, Marcy [OH-9]
Rep Lee, Barbara [CA-9]
Rep McDermott, Jim [WA-7]
Rep Moran, James P. [VA-8]

Rep Owens, Major R. [NY-11]
Rep Sanders, Bernard [VT]
Rep Schakowsky, Janice D. [IL-9]
Rep Slaughter, Louise McIntosh [NY-28]
Rep Solis, Hilda L. [CA-32]
Rep Stark, Fortney Pete [CA-13]
Rep Waters, Maxine [CA-35]
Rep Watson, Diane E. [CA-33]
Rep Woolsey, Lynn C. [CA-6]

THE BILL OF RIGHTS

Amendments 1-10 of the
United States Constitution

The Conventions of a number of the States having, at the time of adopting the Constitution, expressed a desire, in order to prevent misconstruction or abuse of its powers, that further declaratory and restrictive clauses should be added, and as extending the ground of public confidence in the Government will best insure the beneficent ends of its institution;

Resolved, by the Senate and House of Representatives of the United States of America, in Congress assembled, two-thirds of both Houses concurring, that the following articles be proposed to the Legislatures of the several States, as amendments to the Constitution of the United States; all or any of which articles, when ratified by three-fourths of the said Legislatures, to be valid to all intents and purposes as part of the said Constitution, namely:

Amendment I

Congress shall make no law respecting an establishment of religion, or prohibiting the free exercise thereof; or *abridging the freedom of speech, or of the press*; or the right of the people peaceably to assemble, and to petition the government for a redress of grievances.

Amendment II

A well regulated militia, being necessary to the security of a free state, the right of the people to keep and bear arms, shall not be infringed.

Amendment III

No soldier shall, in time of peace be quartered in any house, without the consent of the owner, nor in time of war, but in a manner to be prescribed by law.

Amendment IV

The right of the people to be secure in their persons, houses, papers, and effects, against unreasonable searches and seizures, shall not be violated, and no warrants shall issue, but upon probable cause, supported by oath or affirmation, and particularly describing the place to be searched, and the persons or things to be seized.

Amendment V

No person shall be held to answer for a capital, or otherwise infamous crime, unless on a presentment or indictment of a grand jury, except in cases arising in the land or naval forces, or in the militia, when in actual service in time of war or public danger; nor shall any person be subject for the same offense to be twice put in jeopardy of life or limb; nor shall be compelled in any criminal case to be a witness against himself, nor be deprived of life, liberty, or property, without due process of law; nor shall private property be taken for public use, without just compensation.

Amendment VI

In all criminal prosecutions, the accused shall enjoy the right to a speedy and public trial, by an impartial jury of the state and district wherein the crime shall have been committed, which district shall have been previously ascertained by law, and to be informed of the nature and cause of the accusation; to be confronted with the witnesses against him; to have compulsory process for obtaining witnesses in his favor, and to have the assistance of counsel for his defense.

Amendment VII

In suits at common law, where the value in controversy shall exceed twenty dollars, the right of trial by jury shall be preserved, and no fact tried by a jury, shall be otherwise reexamined in any court of the United States, than according to the rules of the common law.

Amendment VIII

Excessive bail shall not be required, nor excessive fines imposed, nor cruel and unusual punishments inflicted.

Amendment IX

The enumeration in the Constitution, of certain rights, shall not be construed to deny or disparage others retained by the people.

Amendment X

The powers not delegated to the United States by the Constitution, nor prohibited by it to the states, are reserved to the states respectively, or to the people.

The Federal
Communications
Commission Members

Biography of
FCC Chairman
Kevin J. Martin

Kevin J. Martin is Chairman of the FCC. He was nominated to be a member of the Federal Communications Commission by President George W. Bush on April 30, 2001, and was sworn in on July 3, 2001. Chairman Martin was re-nominated for a second term as commissioner and chairman by President George W. Bush on April 25, 2006.

Chairman Martin joined the Commission from the White House, where he served as a Special Assistant to the President for Economic Policy and was on the staff of the National Economic Council. In that capacity, he focused primarily on commerce and technology policy issues. He also served as the official U.S. government representative to the G-8's Digital Opportunity Task Force, a government non-profit, and private sector task force created to identify ways in which the digital revolution can assure opportunities for developing countries.

Prior to joining the Bush Administration, Chairman Martin served as a technology and telecommunications advisor on the Bush-Cheney Transition team. He assumed this role after serving as the Deputy General Counsel to the Bush campaign in Austin, Texas from July 1999 through December 2000.

From 1997 to 1999, Chairman Martin served as a Legal Advisor to FCC Commissioner Harold Furchtgott-Roth, advising the Commissioner on telecommunications and broadband issues. Chairman Martin had previously served in the Office of the Independent Counsel following several years of work in private practice at the Washington, DC law firm of Wiley, Rein & Fielding. While at Wiley, Rein & Fielding, he worked on communications, legislative, and appellate litigation matters. Before joining Wiley, Rein & Fielding, Martin was a law clerk for United States Court District Judge William M. Hoeveler in Miami, Florida.

Chairman Martin received a Bachelor of Arts in Political Science from the University of North Carolina and earned a Masters in Public Policy from Duke University and a J.D. from Harvard Law School. Chairman Martin is a member of the District of Columbia Bar and the Federal Communications Bar Association.

Martin currently resides in Washington, DC with his wife, Catherine Jurgensmeyer Martin, and his sons Luke and William.

Biography of
FCC Commissioner
Michael J. Copps

Michael J. Copps was sworn in for his first term as a member of the Federal Communications Commission on May 31, 2001. He was nominated for a second term on November 9, 2005, and sworn in January 3, 2006. His current term runs until June 30, 2010.

Mr. Copps served from 1998 until January 2001 as Assistant Secretary of Commerce for Trade Development at the U.S. Department of Commerce. In that role, Mr. Copps worked to improve market access and market share for nearly every sector of American industry, including information technologies and telecommunications. Mr. Copps devoted much of his time to building private sector-public sector partnerships to enhance our nation's success in the global economy.

From 1993 to 1998, Mr. Copps served as Deputy Assistant Secretary for Basic Industries, a component of the Trade Development Unit.

Mr. Copps moved to Washington in 1970, joined the staff of Senator Fritz Hollings (D-SC) and served for over a dozen years as Administrative Assistant and Chief of Staff. From 1985 to 1989, he served as Director of Government Affairs for a Fortune 500 Company. From 1989 to 1993, he was Senior Vice President for Legislative Affairs at a major national trade association.

Mr. Copps, a native of Milwaukee, Wisconsin, received a B.A. from Wofford College and earned a Ph.D. in United States history from the University of North Carolina at Chapel Hill. He taught U.S. history at Loyola University of the South from 1967 to 1970.

Copps is married to the former Elizabeth Catherine Miller of New Orleans. They have five children and reside in Alexandria, VA.

Biography of
FCC Commissioner
Jonathan S. Adelstein

Jonathan S. Adelstein was sworn in as a member of the Federal Communications Commission on December 3, 2002, and sworn in for a new five-year term on December 6, 2004.

Before joining the FCC, Adelstein served for fifteen years as a staff member in the United States Senate. For the last seven years, he was a senior legislative aide to United States Senate Majority Leader Tom Daschle (D-SD), where he advised Senator Daschle on telecommunications, financial services, transportation and other key issues. Previously, he served as Professional Staff Member to Senate Special Committee on Aging Chairman David Pryor (D-AR), including an assignment as a special liaison to Senator Harry Reid (D-NV), and as a Legislative Assistant to Senator Donald W. Riegle, Jr. (D-MI).

Prior to his service in the Senate, Adelstein held a number of academic positions, including: Teaching Fellow in the Department of History, Harvard University; Teaching Assistant in the Department of History, Stanford University; and Communications Consultant to the Stanford University Graduate School of Business.

Adelstein received a B.A. in Political Science from Stanford University, an M.A. in History from Stanford University; studied at the Kennedy School of Government at Harvard University; and is a graduate of Phillips

Academy in Andover, Massachusetts. He is a member of the National Academy of Social Insurance, the Phi Kappa Phi National Honor Society and the Pi Sigma Alpha Political Science Honor Society.

Adelstein was born and raised in Rapid City, South Dakota. He now lives in the Washington, D.C. area with his wife Karen, son Adam, and daughter Lexi.

Biography of
FCC Commissioner
Deborah Taylor Tate

Deborah Taylor Tate was nominated to the Federal Communications Commission by President George W. Bush on November 9, 2005 and unanimously confirmed by the United States Senate on December 21, 2005. She was sworn in as FCC Commissioner on January 3, 2006. Among her many responsibilities, Commissioner Tate serves as Chair of both the Federal-State Joint Board on Universal Service (Universal Service Joint Board) and the Federal-State Joint Board on Jurisdictional Separations.

Commissioner Tate has worked extensively to facilitate market-based solutions to public policy issues. Drawing on her extensive experience at the state and local level, Commissioner Tate actively promotes cooperative federalism and public/private partnerships when it is time for the government to act. And, as a leading voice on issues affecting families and children, she has been at the forefront of the movement to ensure that advances in communications technologies benefit all Americans.

At the time of her FCC appointment, Commissioner Tate was serving a six-year term as a Chairman and director of the Tennessee Regulatory Authority. In that position, she had been appointed by the Chairman of the FCC to the Federal-State Joint Board on Advanced Telecommunications Services and was already actively engaged in DC on both telecom and energy issues as Chairman of the Washington

Action Committee for NARUC. Commissioner Tate also is a member of several bar associations and a Rule 31 Mediator.

Commissioner Tate has been an adjunct lecturer at the MBA, Nursing and Law School level and served as a Director at Vanderbilt's Institute on Public Policy. Commissioner Tate formerly served as Legal Counsel and senior policy advisor to two Governors: then Governor (now U.S. Senator) Lamar Alexander and former Governor and Congressman Don Sundquist. In that capacity, Commissioner Tate addressed a diverse array of public policy issues, including attracting new industries and improving family incomes. Commissioner Tate also was instrumental in the creation and implementation of a Mental Health Commissioner, culminating in the passage of a comprehensive mental health law for Tennessee.

Commissioner Tate speaks regularly at law schools, nonprofits and professional organizations across the country, seeking to inspire others through her lifelong commitment to volunteerism. She is the founder and former president of Renewal House, a recovery residence for women addicted to crack cocaine. Commissioner Tate is currently chair of board of directors of Centerstone, Tennessee's largest behavioral healthcare organization. Her board service has included positions on the boards of the Vanderbilt Children's Hospital, Martha O'Bryan Center Foundation, Tennessee Voices for Children, Tennessee Tomorrow, Inc., and League of Women Voters. She and her husband, William H. Tate, a Nashville attorney, have three college age children.

Biography of
FCC Commissioner
Robert M. McDowell

Robert M. McDowell was nominated by President George W. Bush to a seat on the Federal Communications Commission on February 6, 2006, for the remainder of the term expiring June 30, 2009. He was unanimously confirmed by the United States Senate on May 26, 2006, and sworn in as FCC Commissioner on June 1, 2006.

Commissioner McDowell brings to the FCC approximately sixteen years of private sector experience in the communications industry. Immediately prior to joining the FCC, Commissioner McDowell was senior vice president and assistant general counsel for COMPTEL, an association representing competitive facilities-based telecommunications service providers, emerging VoIP providers, integrated communications companies, and their supplier partners, where he had responsibilities involving advocacy efforts before Congress, the White House and executive agencies. He has served on the North American Numbering Council (NANC) and on the board of directors of North American Numbering Plan Billing and Collection, Inc. (NBANC).

Prior to joining COMPTEL in February 1999, McDowell served as the executive vice president and general counsel of America's Carriers Telecommunications Association (ACTA), which merged with COMPTEL at that time.

McDowell was graduated cum laude from Duke University in 1985. After serving as chief legislative aide to a member of the Virginia House of Delegates, he attended the Marshall-Wythe School of Law at the College of William and Mary. Upon his graduation from law school, McDowell joined the Washington, D.C., office of Arter & Hadden, a national law firm based in Cleveland.

Extensively involved in civic and political affairs, McDowell has served on numerous boards and commissions. He was appointed by Virginia Governor George Allen to the Governor's Advisory Board for a Safe and Drug-Free Virginia, and to the Virginia Board for Contractors, to which he was reappointed by Governor Jim Gilmore. A veteran of several presidential campaigns, he was counsel to the Bush-Cheney Florida Recount Team in 2000. His work during the 1992 presidential campaign is cited in the Almanac of American Politics, 1994. Among his other endeavors, McDowell has twice been a candidate for the Virginia General Assembly. He currently serves as Chairman of the Board of the McLean Project for the Arts.

McDowell is admitted to practice law before the courts of the Commonwealth of Virginia, the U.S. District Court for the Eastern District of Virginia, the U.S. Courts of Appeals for the District of Columbia, First, Fourth and Fifth Circuits and the U.S. Supreme Court. He resides in Fairfax County, Va., on the farm where he grew up, with his wife Jennifer and their three children.

ABOUT THE AUTHOR

D r. Kenneth C. Hill has been active in communications and broadcasting all of his adult life, having been involved for over three decades in virtually every aspect of television and radio—from sales, programming, sports broadcasting, news, and weather reporting in his earlier years—to planning and general supervision and management of non-commercial, educational and commercial radio facilities; and in the construction and supervision of campus radio facilities and off-campus radio and television productions.

His broadcasting and communications career has included teaching at the college level in the areas of mass communication, television and radio production, film production, broadcast journalism, public speaking, principles of advertising and broadcast management, and numerous other subjects in the communications/broadcasting field.

Dr. Hill has also provided consulting and contract services for over two decades in the areas of technical writing and editing, public relations, proposal writing and editing, independent R&D documentation, corporate and business communication, media acquisition, media appraisal and media utilization.

Dr. Hill's educational achievements include a Bachelor of Science degree in Speech (Broadcasting) and History - East Tennessee State University; Master of Science Degree in Speech (Broadcasting) – Indiana State University; Bachelor of Arts degree in Biblical Studies – Baptist Christian College; Master of Religious Education – Manahath School of Theology; and Doctor of Religious Education – Andersonville Baptist Seminary.

For the past twenty-six years, Dr. Hill has been affiliated with the Appalachian Educational Communication Corporation (AECC) Bristol, Tennessee and is currently Chief Executive Officer and serves as General Manager of five radio stations reaching portions of five states in the Eastern United States. As such, he is responsible for the planning and oversight of operations for those stations and for planning and execution of educational programs, as well as programs of a general nature at the corporation's historic Cameo Theatre.

As an ordained Minister of The Evangelical Methodist Church, Dr. Hill has pastored in various churches in Indiana and Tennessee over the past three decades. He has served as Secretary of the General Conference of the Evangelical Methodist Churches for the past 17 years, and is General Director of Siloam International, an independent Christian mission organization. In his years of service to the Church, Dr. Hill has traveled as a missions task force member to Russia, Chile, Central Africa, and Honduras.

Dr. Hill also utilized his broadcast and communications knowledge and experience abroad, serving as a consultant to broadcast station licensees and as a member of the Construction Team for Radio Paz in Nicaragua in 2002 and as Construction Coordinator of Radio Renovacion Biblico Templo in Honduras in 1992.

Other Current Activities

-- Board Member: Bancroft Gospel Ministry, Alpha/Omega Ministries, and Breckbill Bible College

-- Chairman of Publications Board of The Evangelical Methodist Church

-- Owner of WMCH Radio, Inc., serving the Tri-Cities area of Tennessee and Virginia (Kingsport/Bristol/Johnson City) with Christian programming.

-- Speaker on "The Scripture Speaks" Radio Broadcast.

-- Rule 31 General and Civil Mediator and Family Mediator of the Tennessee Supreme Court.

-- Member, Tennessee State Republican Party Executive Committee

-- Member, Bristol Evening Lions Club

-- Vice-President and Board of Trustees of Southwest Radio Church of the Air

-- Tri-Cities Mass Choir. Member, Board of Directors

-- Board of Directors, Virginia Association of Broadcasters.

Dr. Hill has written, co-authored, and edited a number of books, including Prayers Jabez Didn't Pray (Hearthstone Publishing), A Classic Christmas, (Appalachian Family Publications), Constitution in Crisis – two editions (Hearthstone Publishing), and Constitution Conspiracy (Hearthstone Publishing). He has also written articles for Religious Broadcasting magazine.

The author has produced an array of Christian educational materials, both video and audio, on such subjects as Holy Land sites, Christian history, Scripture, and Prophecy.

Dr. Hill has been listed in Who's Who Among Rising Young Americans (1992); Who's Who in Religion (1992-2007); Who's Who in the South and Southwest (1993-2007); and Who's Who in the World (1994-2007)

Dr. Hill is married and lives with his wife, Janet, in the mountains of East Tennessee. The couple has three children.